exploring

VISUAL
STORYTELLING

*Brian Arnold &
Brendan Eddy*

DESIGN
EXPLORATION
SERIES

THOMSON

DELMAR LEARNING   Australia Canada Mexico Singapore Spain United Kingdom United States

THOMSON

DELMAR LEARNING

Exploring Visual Storytelling
By Brian Arnold and Brendan Eddy

Vice President, Technology and Trades Business Unit:
Dave Garza

Editorial Director:
Sandy Clark

Senior Acquisitions Editor:
James Gish

Product Managers:
Jaimie Weiss
Molly Belmont

Editorial Assistant:
Niamh Matthews

Marketing Director:
Deborah Yarnell

Marketing Coordinator:
Shanna Gibbs

Production Director:
Patty Stephan

Managing Editor:
Larry Main

Production Manager:
Stacy Masucci

Production Editor:
Andrea Majot

Technology Project Manager:
Kevin Smith

Cover Design:
Steven Brower

Cover Image:
Brendan Eddy and Julia Belgum

Library of Congress Cataloging-in-Publication Data

Arnold, Brian.
 Exploring visual storytelling / by Brian Arnold and Brendan Eddy.
  p. cm.
 ISBN-13: 978-1-4180-1492-6
 ISBN-10: 1-4180-1492-3
 1. Motion picture authorship. 2. Television authorship. 3. Visual communication. I. Eddy, Brendan. II. Title.
 PN1996.A75 2007
 808'.066791—dc22
              2007005465

NOTICE TO THE READER

contents

preface

How to use this text and DVD

Format and Cross-Reference ability

The process of learning to tell compelling visual stories is not linear. The concepts, skills, and tools mastered in pursuit of visual storytelling are not acquired in a series of well-defined steps; rather, they are absorbed through practice and familiarity. There are too many variables involved in visual storytelling for a linear system to work for all people. Familiarity with all the ideas in this textbook and DVD will be invaluable to you in your pursuit of compelling work; however, that does not mean that this book should be read as if it were a narrative and then practiced perfectly the next moment. This textbook/DVD is intended to be your companion as you climb the slippery slope of visual storytelling to the peak of mastery. The ideas contained herein should be considered in small steps, practiced, and wrestled with; then when you are comfortable with the content, new areas should be explored.

This text is designed with nonlinear usability in mind. The chapters build on each other; however, great quantities of standalone information are contained in each section for quick reference and reminders. The textbook is also intended to be used in conjunction with the DVD, which has an interface that is similarly designed to allow a nonlinear access, essentially letting the user decide the order in which content is viewed. Each chapter in the book corresponds to a section of the DVD while most of the principles contained in this text can be used to analyze virtually any part of the DVD.

Unless you relegate *Exploring Visual Storytelling* to the bookshelf full of tomes you know you should get to, but never really muster the effort to read, then there is no wrong way to use it. Keep in mind that no skill can be truly acquired without reinforcing practice. Visual storytelling is no exception, so make it a habit and keep it a skill.

Quotes

The quotes at the beginning of each chapter set the tone for the chapter and take the ideas contained within to a more global level of consideration. You are encouraged to revisit the quotes *after* completing each chapter.

Key Terms

Each key term will be listed at the beginning of each chapter, bolded when it first occurs in the text, and listed at the end in the glossary. Mastery of concepts begins with a common language. Many of the terms used in visual storytelling have alternate meanings outside the realm of visual storytelling, so it behooves us all to have a common vocabulary as a starting point for clear communication and learning.

Key Questions

Key questions are listed near the end of each chapter. The questions encourage discussion of the most important ideas contained in each chapter and allow for self-assessment.

Summary

The summary of each chapter occurs at the end and helps the user to tie the concepts together; it serves as an excellent quick reference when the user is looking for a review of the material.

Exercises

The exercises at the end of each chapter are there to encourage you to get your hands dirty with the new concepts. The tools and ideas contained in *Exploring Visual Storytelling* are only useful in their application, not as untried (by you) theory. So, once you have read a chapter, take your best shot at the exercises to prove to yourself that you have mastered the content.

TARGET AUDIENCE FOR THIS BOOK

- First year visual arts students who need a reference companion to integrate all the ideas inherent in their curriculum
- This book is for prose writers! This book is about telling visual stories. Audiences today expect visual stories on screens and in their books. The only difference between visual storytelling for the screen and the page is that the prose writer must illustrate with language what the screenwriter expects to show on screen.
- People interested in the visual arts but unsure how to begin
- Working professionals in the entertainment industries who understand the need to broaden their skills
- Teachers who need to engage a class with the presentation of material
- Leaders and managers who need to hold the attention of their audience in meetings
- Anyone who looks over the fence between the visual and the story side of entertainment at the greener grass on the other side
- Hobbyists ready to make the transition to professional
- People who feel that their skill set is unbalanced in relation to storytelling
- Advertising creatives
- Sales people who need to pitch
- Storyboard artists
- Writers
- Independent film makers

These are timeless ideas independent of trends and technology.

DESIGN EXPLORATION SERIES

Exploring Visual Storytelling is part of the growing Design Exploration Series published by Thomson Delmar Learning as well as the first of the published materials from Visual Culture. This format of user-controlled textbook/DVD could easily be the basis for a series of books on a wide variety of subjects.

WHY WE WROTE *EXPLORING VISUAL STORYTELLING*

We created *Exploring Visual Storytelling* first and foremost because it represents our greatest passion, creating a culture of visual storytellers. We worked together on a variety of independent projects over the last few years, each more elaborate than the last, and we knew we wanted to do something in the visual arts that utilized directing abilities and 3-D animation skills and at the same time demonstrated story/writing skills. With nothing but an unwavering belief in our eventual success, Brendan took out a second mortgage on his house and we both poured all our spare time into creating the first Visual Storytelling DVD. Three bleary eyed months later, Visual Storytelling, a DVD that clearly articulated the tools necessary to become a compelling visual storyteller, was born.

During this process a fellow visionary named Neil Hagre stepped forward and lent his considerable web design skills to our first professional looking website. Product in hand and URL firmly established, we were on our way. All we lacked was distribution. Cue sitcom wah-wahh sound effect. If you have ever lacked distribution, you can appreciate the enormity of our dilemma.

So we set up a print on demand deal with CustomFlix® and took out ad space on a national animation website. Within no time we peaked out with vaguely mediocre sales whose revenue failed to even cover the cost of the advertising. Distribution, hmm.... Not the most auspicious beginning, and we were in a real pinch. So, assuming that luck favors the prepared, we sent our complete DVD to several publishers and hoped for the best. Lucky for us, "the best" is exactly what we got. In our case the best took the form of James Gish, Acquisitions Editor from Thomson Delmar Learning.

James viewed our DVD and quickly gave us a call during which he encouraged us to share our vision for the project. We elaborated on our goals and pointed out places on the DVD where it could have been even better if we had more financial and editorial assistance. Jim listened patiently, asked a series of insightful questions, and then disappeared. Surfacing occasionally over the next six months with phone calls, contracts, and then proposals, Jim finessed *Exploring Visual Storytelling* into an official Thomson project. We now had backing to create a textbook and more elaborate DVD. The icing on the cake was, of course, that we now had distribution. Cue trumpets of triumph!

Now, both Visual Culture and Thomson Delmar Learning share a common vision for *Exploring Visual Storytelling*: a DVD/textbook companion to serve as a future paradigm for media related textbooks where a DVD accompaniment is not the exception, but the rule. The next few years will reveal the truth of our convictions; as for you, please read, watch, and discuss.

CONCEPTUAL DESIGN OF THIS TEXT

This textbook/DVD companion set is designed for both linear and nonlinear access. The arrangement allows the viewer to experience the information in a clear and coherent manner, while providing modular subject matter that stands alone and supplements other areas of exploration. The goal is to arrive at a format that is user friendly for the novice looking to get an overview and quick to reference for a more experienced visual storyteller looking for answers to specific problems.

The textbook chapters are designed to coincide with the DVD's clear and succinct illustration of concepts in a way that reinforces the material of the DVD and elaborates on the topics at greater depth. The magic of the DVD is that no matter how clear the explanation of a visual concept, it is never entirely clear without a concrete positive example to view. Think of the DVD as a touchstone for understanding and discussion of all the topics covered in the textbook.

There are hundreds of books on the art of story writing and nearly the same amount of books about capturing visuals for a story, but there seems to be precious few books that capture the idea from brainstorming to execution and present it in clear, simple terms. *Exploring Visual Storytelling* fills the market needs for a novice, hobbyist, college student in a media arts program, and professional interested in an overview of the principles that make interesting and compelling stories for people to watch.

Any student in his or her first year of a media arts program will find *Exploring Visual Storytelling* an essential tool in assimilating all the technical and conceptual ideas contained in introductory courses. *Exploring Visual Storytelling* also acts as a filtering agent and source of context for the technical side of the visual arts.

Many industry artists and visual specialists are frustrated by their inability to master compelling storytelling, especially in its relation to the visuals. *Exploring Visual Storytelling* addresses this frustration and provides concrete tools to bridge their knowledge and experiential gap.

Visual arts hobbyists and paraprofessionals who are ready to take their art and craft from good to greatness and sincere impact are well armed with *Exploring Visual Storytelling* because it outlines the steps necessary to organize great ideas into great visual stories.

ABOUT THE AUTHORS

Brian Arnold Co-founder of Visual Culture, Brian earned his Master of Fine Arts in Screenwriting from the University of Southern California School of Cinema and Television. He is the author of several feature film screenplays, and founder and head of the successful Los Angeles based Play Onwards Writers Group.

Brian worked at Nickelodeon Animation Studios in Burbank, California, for five years during which time he participated in a wide range of popular children's television animation. As an editor, Brian was responsible for every aspect of the "character and story" process, contributing to the processes in everything from pilot episodes and direct to video projects to theatrical releases. Titles Brian worked on include: *Invader Zim, Spongebob Squarepants, Hey Arnold!, Catdog, Angry Beavers, Oswald*, and *Dora the Explorer*.

Since 2002, Brian has—while contributing to Visual Culture—worked for the Art Institutes, currently as the Dean of Academic Affairs at the Art Institute California Design College campus.

Brendan Eddy After completing his first animated short film in 1994, Brendan enrolled in Minneapolis College of Art and Design and received both of its merit-based scholarships. While attending classes he also worked as a teaching assistant for a variety of animation and computer classes and as a freelance animator and editor. In March 1998, Brendan completed a short film that was featured in two film festivals, the Rough and Ruined and the Black Chair.

Brendan became an instructor at the Minnesota School of Computer Imaging (MSCI) in 1998. Within six months he was promoted to Director of Digital Production for MSCI's animation department. In this role, he designed the majority of the animation department's curriculum and set up and administered the school's computer network. During his MSCI tenure, he taught virtually every class in the program, hired and managed faculty and staff, and co-directed scheduling, career placement, and admission of the student body. He attained the highest career placement percentage in the history of the department.

In 2000, Brendan became a fulltime freelance animator working on multiple projects including television series development, feature films, and commercial projects. His responsibilities included animator, illustrator, producer, and project manager. Brendan became an instructor at the Art Institutes International Minnesota in 2001 where he repeatedly received the highest evaluations from both the administration and students. He continues to act in an advisory capacity at both the Art Institute and M.S.C.I.

In his capacity as both a working animator and an educator he has witnessed firsthand the challenges involved in creating animated stories of both quality and substance. With this expertise he started Visual Culture in 2003.

ACKNOWLEDGEMENTS

We would like to acknowledge the tireless support and relentless dedication of the following people at Thomson Delmar: James Gish, Jaimie Weiss, Niamh Matthews, and Molly Belmont. For going above and beyond the call of duty in support of Visual Culture we would like to express endless thanks to: Neil Hagre, Tom and Helen Eddy, Amy and Rachel Arnold, Myron and Judy Arnold, and the fabulous interns—who systematically got hired away.

DEDICATION

Exploring Visual Storytelling is dedicated to creating a strong visual culture.

TO THE READER

Our goal in creating *Exploring Visual Storytelling* is to create a user-controlled experience: an interface that works best for you. You may find it easiest and most rewarding to watch the DVD all the way though before skimming chapters to find areas of great question or you may wish to view one DVD chapter at a time with the book open to the corresponding text chapter. Review of either the text or the DVD enriches your experience of the other. The experience is intended to be integrated an immersive.

Exploring Visual Storytelling specifically omits detailed reference to audio; this is not to minimize its importance so much as to encapsulate it in the larger principles. Audio is tremendously important and most of the basic principles of this text can be applied to sound.

Learning styles and attention spans vary. Our goal is to provide you with materials that are nonlinear and principles that are timeless. The more energy you invest in the material the greater your comprehension and application skills will grow. Discreet viewing of sections will yield knowledge, but deeper understanding always comes with greater depth of exploration. The principles of *Exploring Visual Storytelling* transcend trends, medium, and genre. So flip though, fast forward, or dive in and explore; it's all here waiting for you.

The purpose of *Exploring Visual Storytelling* is not to provide the one and only way to create great work. Investment of your time combined with these principles is a reasonable way to increase the odds of your great idea evolving into compelling stories. This companion set is about arming you with the most widely used and clearly explained tools of the trade.

SPECIAL FEATURES

▶ Objectives

Learning objectives start off each chapter. They describe the competencies the reader should achieve upon understanding the chapter material.

▶ Key Terms

Key terms at the beginning of each chapter introduce readers to the new terminology they will come across within the chapter.

▶ In Review

Review questions are located at the end of each chapter and allow readers to assess their understanding of the chapter.

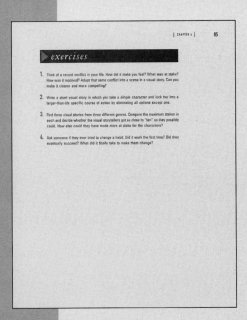

▶ Exercises

Projects are located at the end of the chapter and help reinforce chapter material through practical applications.

▶ Figures

The art program is based largely on the accompanying back-of-book DVD film. These figures tie concepts in the chapter directly to specific places in the film, helping promote a direct connection between the book and film.

CHAPTER 1

"The whole story of the universe is implicit in any part of it. The meditative eye can look through any single object and see, as through a window, the entire cosmos."

—Aldous Huxley (1894–1963)

objectives

- Define visual storytelling
- Distinguish between talent and passion
- Identify rationale for audience engagement
- Establish the foundational elements of visual storytelling
- Explain the benefits of the pre-production process
- Discuss tools for story creation

key terms

story	main character	pre-production	script
visual storytelling	obstacles	production	shot list
talent	decision	post-production	storyboards
passion	realization	brainstorming	primary element
audience	contrast	concept-forming	pitching
catharsis	nonlinear	outline	story beat

INTRODUCTION TO VISUAL STORYTELLING

Mention of storytelling triggers memories of elementary school and Renaissance festivals for many people. Storytelling, however, is more than a childhood experience. Storytelling is the root of information recording and the medium upon which all other media rely for successful communication and retention. In this textbook, the term **story** refers to a fictional narrative intended to communicate ideas and feelings in a compelling manner. As such, **visual storytelling** is the craft of using images to create a fictional but believable reality that fulfills the intended audience's expectations.

While the "visual" element of visual storytelling relies on the principles by which the artist makes stylistic decisions for creating characters, actions, and backgrounds, the craft of storytelling is also governed by a series of rules and guidelines. The first five chapters address story construction; pre-production, context, character, conflict, and plot. In Chapter 6 through Chapter 9, you will learn how to apply artistic components to your story using space and time, two- and three-dimensional space, and staging. Chapter 10 provides story-shaping tools and revisits brainstorming to help you apply what you have learned to the storytelling process.

NOTE

Rules are tools. Rules help to guide and shape the structure of stories, enabling visual storytellers to craft clear and compelling tales from nothing more than their imaginations. As tools, rules are not to be obeyed at the expense of a compelling story. If a good story needs to break a rule, then so be it.

As with the foundations of drawing and perspective, the principles of story construction lead the visual storyteller through a maze of pitfalls that may otherwise prevent a great concept from evolving into a well-executed presentation. And as with drawing, the craft of visual storytelling revolves around principles that can be learned through study and application. The art of visual storytelling, however, comes to life only through realization of the visual storyteller's unique vision of the world. The art of visual storytelling lies in the execution of the idea, not the idea itself. It resides in the style and perspective in which a visual story is told, not in the list of events that take place. Two visual stories may share similar plot, character types, or location premises, yet the stories themselves be completely dissimilar. The art of visual storytelling–the distinctive style of each artist–differentiates one story from the next.

The audience does not remember what happens in a visual story as much as the execution of those happenings. Because of this phenomenon, the way in which the story is told (the tone, perspective, and insight) makes the difference between an audience exclaiming "It was genius!" and droning "How trite" in reaction to a story. People perceive events from an infinite variety of perspectives making it possible for every visual story to have a unique flavor.

Through careful study of the craft of visual storytelling, the visual storyteller is able to present a story that reveals something genuine about life. When the audience responds to this revelation, there is art. Therefore, a visual storyteller must strive for art by carefully sharing his unique worldview while simultaneously revealing a basic human truth.

Storytelling is more about execution than ideas. Many stories share the same core events, locations and character types. The value to the audience is not in the idea for the story but in the unique and interesting way in which the visual storyteller brings it to life on the screen.

figure | 1–1 |

When a visual storyteller reveals basic human truths by bringing a unique perspective to a story, there is art.

TALENT AND PASSION

Through multimedia infused with periodic humor, *Exploring Visual Storytelling* helps students lay the framework for compelling visual stories by examining the principles, rules, and examples that comprise the craft of visual storytelling. This textbook takes students down a clear path leading from murky ideas to sharply executed entertainment. To best introduce this craft, it must be restated that each visual storyteller brings a unique perspective to the story drawing board. Your perspective is not found through careful study or late-night cram sessions, but rather it is born from something personal: talent and passion.

Talent is a special, often creative or artistic aptitude, synonymous with a basal ability to properly complete a task the first time. Everyone has some form of talent, be it drawing, writing, animating, editing–even skateboarding down a staircase. People who practice their talents develop skills. The stronger a person's talent is at the outset, the greater the likelihood that the acquired skills will be impressive. A person can, of course, gain substantial skills in an area where there is little talent, but the journey is more difficult and the likelihood of quick or notable success is much lower.

Most successful people are motivated to improve their talents. Successful visual storytellers find their motivation in some form of their passions. **Passion** is the motivated and caring aspect applied to one's talent. It is the level of attraction a person

figure | 1–2 |

Talent comes in a variety of forms.

holds for any given task and what drives him toward his goals. Passion is reflected in the amount of time a person spends thinking about his talent when he is not using it. People have passion for the challenges and ideas that are ever present in their minds– while driving, eating dinner, or sitting in class. When a talented person's mind wanders, it usually heads for his passions. What is the first thing you think of as you wake up, and the last thing you think of as you fall asleep?

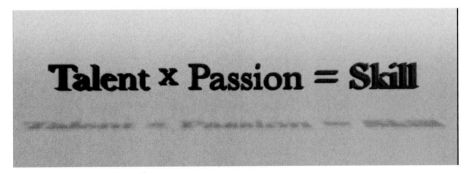

figure | 1–3 |

Your passion is talent's multiplier.

figure | 1–4 |

Mongo has a passion for the goal.

Since experiences dictate the stories we tell, it is crucial that the visual storyteller understand his passions, in order to seek out the types of visual stories that feed his passions and avoid the ones that do not. Employing creativity is hard work, so your best shot at using creativity well is to be passionate about it. Then, you will have the continuous energy to take even the most difficult of steps necessary to create a well-polished product. When following your passions, no activity feels like work.

So, how are passions acquired? Passions reside in each of us, waiting for serious self-assessment and honesty to unlock them. An artist must ask himself what he cares about most. The answer to this question informs the shape of his passions. The following diagnostics will help you identify your passions:

1. You start working on something, and hours pass by in what feels like a moment to you.

2. Musicians talk about something called a "player's high." It is a state where they have so completely lost themselves in the act of creating music that the instrument and the notes and all the tangible trappings of making music fade away, while the

musician simply "becomes" the music. At any point where you are creating art, if you can transcend the tools and simply exist in the medium, you have found a passion.

3. Someone offers you a chance to do something "fun" by conventional standards, and you ditch it to do something else: your passion.

4. There is a subject (your passion) that you talk about so much that other people know you as "that person who talks about X."

5. You only feel truly satisfied if you have spent time every day doing this one thing.

figure | 1–5 |

When passion is involved, the process feeds on itself.

A visual storyteller must ask himself, "What excites me each day?" It does not matter whether it is racecars, rockets, or data-entry accounting; the important aspect of the activity that generates your excitement is that it makes the *visual storyteller* passionate. This self-assessment requires committed honesty and repeated examination: if balancing columns of numbers is a taste of heaven for the visual storyteller, than he must admit it as a passion, regardless of how other people feel about the subject.

Both the art and craft of visual storytelling allow room for passions across the spectrum. For example, many people would give anything to spend a day on a movie set. Cameraman, boom operator, gaffer, director–these are highly coveted positions for many people really passionate about those jobs and who desire to be a part of those processes. However, for people who have passions other than these, a day spent on production is like a trip to the dentist for a root canal. Simply put: if one man's trash is

figure | 1–6 |

In order to achieve a goal there must be passion for it.

another man's treasure, then surely one man's passion is another man's torture. To each his own. The most important thing to remember is to be honest with yourself about your own passions.

figure | 1–7 |

People who are honest about their goals are best able to attain them.

Being passionate does not mean that every good visual storyteller needs to be madly in love with scriptwriting in order to create a compelling visual story. Still, the trick is to stir up genuine excitement about writing by finding the areas of visual storytelling that *do* interest you, and then allowing them to fuel your excitement for the other steps of the visual storytelling process. When you find these ideas, hold them close for the times when the road gets hard and the work gets long.

Many people believe that being passionate about something requires action at all times. It is true that the more a person participates in a task, the better he becomes at performing it. However, being passionate about something does not necessarily look like something productive to an observer. Creativity requires thought; real thought that is deep and complex and time-consuming. While thinking does not always look productive, it is essential to the creative process, so the visual storyteller needs to be able to find a place for daydreaming, staring out the window, and imagining the impossible.

figure | 1–8 |

Daydreaming nourishes productive storytelling.

There is, of course, a critical next step after daydreaming, one that turns the imagination-cultivating into a concrete activity, namely, that of application. For an idea to be properly actualized, it has to see the light of day, in the form of spoken word, writing, or an image. "I've got it all in my head" is the cry of the amateur hobbyist, not the budding professional visual storyteller.

Once your ideas are committed to paper, you will have to share them. While exposing your ideas to another set of eyes involves great personal risk, it is far better for an idea to be critiqued as a bad one than to receive no feedback at all. There is nothing as wasteful to an artist as spending much time and effort on a bad idea because he did not have the courage to share it sooner. Most importantly, no matter how hard a visual storyteller attempts to *tell* a story, he must have the eventual goal of allowing someone else to experience his ideas through a visual medium, and this requires that the ideas make it onto paper.

| NOTE |

Until an idea goes from brain to paper, it is not fully formed.

WHY DOES AN AUDIENCE WATCH?

Great visual storytellers harbor the desire to create compelling stories. Yet, the trick to becoming a great visual storyteller lies in finding your passion—and then in sharing it with an audience.

Audiences—of any size or age—want an experience. Any intended viewer of a visual story is considered an **audience**. Depending on the content and execution of a story, audiences will relate to it in different ways. A story that is compelling for a retiree might be boring and slow to a teen, whereas the stories that appeal to a teen may appear frenetic and pointless to the retiree. The group of people that the visual storyteller thinks will best relate to the story is called the target audience or intended audience, and the intended audience is often expressed in terms of story genre, such as the science-fiction genre, drama, or coming-of-age tales.

All audiences bring complex expectations to the screen. They want to experience something compelling, but the exact experience sought after will vary from one audience member to the next. Audiences want to feel included in the events on screen and are empowered to do this when they see something recognizable, such as a relatable character trait or struggle. Paradoxically, they want these traits and struggles presented to them in a familiar, yet new and exciting way, one that intrigues them. Audiences want to be asked questions by a story, but if the audiences' understanding of the story hinges on the answers, they will feel threatened, not challenged. Audiences want questions raised; they do not want to be quizzed as viewers.

Audiences also want to experience a range of strong emotions, which is why some people love seeing romantic comedies while others enjoy horror films or historical epics. An audience evaluates a story's success by the extent to which the story elicits the variety of emotional responses the audience anticipated before viewing. And for people to experience emotions while watching what is, in reality, a flat screen filled with rapidly changing still images, they must feel a link.

Because an audience sits in front of the screen with expectations, those expectations must be rewarded in order to retain the audience's attention. Take note: if a visual storyteller wants to tell a story to serve as personal therapy, then any story can be told for his own benefit; however, do not expect an audience to enjoy the tale. If not carefully crafted with attention paid to the principles and rules of visual storytelling, the audience will not identify with the story. It will know that it was not the intended audience, and that it was not invited to watch a movie so much as got caught watching a long set of travel slides from someone's personal journey.

Visual storytellers must present their own vision of the world based on highly personal experiences, but if there is hope of a captive audience, then the shape of the story needs to cater to the audience's experience during the visual storyteller's presentation of events. As we will emphasize throughout the textbook, this requires preparation, planning, and a great deal of revision under the scrutiny of respected peers and mentors.

Audience members watch the screen in order to feel connected to something larger than their current lives, so that they can experience a catharsis. A **catharsis** is a purification or purgation that releases tension from a person or elicits a spiritual renewal. A visual storyteller knows that to best reach an audience comprised of middle-aged desk jockeys who are frustrated with their bosses, the artist can create a visual story about a relatable character overthrowing oppressive forces in a larger-than-life setting. The audience members can then go home feeling better about their lives–because the viewing allowed them a cathartic experience. Intended audiences, unable to find release for their frustration in their real lives, find fulfillment in watching a character wrestle with the same issues in a fantastic context.

This connection between audience and story is not rooted in a deep emotional bond to a cool visual effect or particularly deft display of martial arts prowess, but a feeling of understanding, even compassion, toward a character. Particularly, intended audience members should be able to connect with the **main character**, the protagonist, or hero of the story, or in some cases, the entity who represents a particular perspective or set of experiences.

Before continuing to discuss the relationship between the audience and characters of a story, we must articulate a key point. No visual story, of any length, topic, or genre, is about an event (the big race), incident (an earthquake), or significant historical episode (fall of the Berlin Wall). Rather, understand that all visual stories are about characters (human, animal, aliens, or personified objects) and their perceptions of and responses to those events, incidents, and episodes–or to *other* characters reacting to those occurrences. The character–not the event or occurrence–is the foundational unit of a visual story, around which all actions, dialogue, and visuals revolve.

Overcoming Obstacles

We know that audiences watch a visual story, so that they can connect with the characters, and we also know that no one wants to stare at a screen for ninety minutes if the characters endure unremarkable lives. If the character and events are considered average, then why make it the subject of a story? There must be some element of above average compelling the audience to watch. Audiences watch a visual story in order to see the character encounter an obstacle, and then witness the character face a realization or decision, in attempts to overcome that obstacle.

Obstacles are roadblocks between the character and the character's goals and can take the form of people, beliefs, geography, or societal expectations. As in real life, the degree to which an obstacle affects a person varies with the importance placed on the goal. Living in a small town might not be an obstacle for a married couple who wants a quiet retirement, but it may be an obstacle for the beautiful woman who wants to become a model. Bullies, oppressive ideologies, cultural expectations–and small towns–are all types of obstacles that elicit the audience's compassion for the afflicted character because viewers want to see the latter overcome the obstacle.

Scenes of Decision or Realization

A good visual story does not allow the main character to solve her problem until she has faced it enough times to have to make a **decision** to change a course of action. Perhaps the model gets her big break and chooses to leave her family, her friends, and everything she knows for the potential of greater reward in the big city, or maybe she resolves to stay in a place she has known forever and invest her efforts in reviving a local ballet studio. Whatever her choice, she was forced to make it because of the obstacles in front of her, and the process of facing the obstacles revealed her values. These values become yet another point at which the audience can relate to the character on screen.

Audiences enjoy these moments because they experience a release when they watch the character they relate to (feel empathically linked to) reach this decision. Real-life decisions often entail onerous or messy consequences, but story decisions allow the audience to entertain a vast array of consequences without actually enduring any ill effects. When the characters make that important decision, the audience can take an emotional risk without suffering potentially disastrous and long-term consequences.

| NOTE |

Visual storytelling choices are clear to the audience and, while emotionally similar to choices in real life, are safe from consequences for the audience.

figure | 1–9 |

Choices are made based on personal values.

Sometimes, a character does not have the ability to make a decision, either because of the circumstances surrounding his situation or because of the nature of the story. In this case, it is vital that the character has a **realization** in which he becomes aware of something profound about his life or in which he reaffirms a belief that is core to his existence. Because the audience relies on a scene of realization to provide emotional satisfaction, much like that taken from a scene of decision, the visual storyteller must compose the scene of realization with great care. In real life realizations are a dime a dozen, while actions resulting from the realization require commitment and focus. The bottom line: if your character is to have a realization, make sure it is compelling for the audience.

Whether your character is prone to simply having or acting on the realization, you must remember that audiences seek out visual stories to partake in a strong emotion. This feeling may be one that they enjoy, or one that they find difficult to experience in their real lives. In either case, the stronger the feelings evoked through the story, the better. When the characters overcome an obstacle, audience members feel that they have also overcome a problem, which allows them to experience catharsis. These feelings of release are difficult to attain outside the visual story and are the primary value for the audience.

SUBTLE TRICKS OF THE TRADE

Most intellectual professionals, from computer programmers to zoologists, employ essential formulas that do not conveniently fit into larger categories of rules. Visual storytelling is no exception, and there are a few applications that great visual storytellers keep in mind at all times.

Contrast

In the visual arts, elements with **contrast** are dynamic and interesting and bring clarity to each other. Homogeneous elements blend together, lessening the value of each involved component. The same is true for stories: if a big, dumb character exists, it is helpful to place him near a small, clever character and use their physical differences to highlight the contrast in their personalities.

Just the same, an opening scene should not contain three brown mice named Joseph, Joey, and Joe. Contrast in all elements, from backgrounds to character names and appearance, clarifies their presentation. If a scene begins on a sad note, it should end happily. If a character wears lots of red, place her in front of a blue background for contrast. If one scene takes place in a submarine, the next should occur in an airplane, train, or spaceship. These opposing elements help the audience to give specific meaning to individual story elements.

figure | 1–10 |

Always emphasize contrast.

Often visual stories that appear to be lacking are simply suffering from too much of one particular element. Not all contrasts need to be exact opposites, but chances are that if a scene feels lackluster, an emphasizing contrast will give it a punch.

Rule of Threes

The rule of threes applies to scenes, characters, and stories. For many reasons, people can easily relate to groups of three, as it instills a sense of balance. Three allows for an introduction to an idea, a reminder thereof, and its placement in long-term memory, then space for either a twist on audience expectation or satisfying resolution. By the same token, three provides a beginning, middle, and end to any structure. The rule of threes plants a habit, elevates it, and then delivers a twist to the habit.

The rule of threes applies to:

- A story

- A scene

- A character's arc (change)

- Any character's attempt to overcome an obstacle

Additionally, there needs to be a beginning, middle, and end (a three) to stories, scenes, a character's arc, and the character's relationship with the obstacle.

And as the adage suggests, three is the magic number–the third time is the charm. A joke is set up (one), reinforced (two), and then twisted or topped to pay it off (three). The third little bear is the one to reinforce Goldilocks' crimes, the oldest (third) Billy Goat Gruff is the one that delivers the blow to the troll, and the two pigs seek refuge in the third's brick house. Characters typically encounter an obstacle once and fail to overcome it. They then try a second time, altering their method and thinking slightly, and fail again. Only when substantial change or force is applied in the third attempt do they arrive at a realization or make a critical decision, which puts them on the path of successful completion of their quest or complete defeat thereof.

Linear and Nonlinear Formats

The story structures discussed in *Exploring Visual Storytelling* follow a linear format, that is, events will happen more or less in chronological order: beginning, middle, and end (incorporating flashbacks or memories appropriately). This is certainly the best way to *learn* how to tell a story, though it is not the *only* way.

Visual stories can be effectively told out of chronological sequence, in a **nonlinear** format, to great effect. This technique requires great skill and experience to avoid stressful production or confusing the audience. Once the concepts in this text are mastered, nonlinear storytelling can offer visual storytellers a delightful place to experiment and express themselves artistically. Or, if it is the experienced visual storyteller's goal, nonlinear storytelling can be used as a method of confusing the audience on purpose.

PRE-PRODUCTION PROCESS

The rule of threes reminds us that a story must have a beginning, middle, and end. We will revisit this concept in several chapters, specifically in Chapter 5, when we explore the three-act story structure. The production of visual stories also falls neatly into three distinct categories analogous to beginnings, middles, and ends: pre-production, production, and post-production.

Pre-production is the detailed planning of the work you will produce. It includes generating and organizing ideas, scriptwriting, storyboarding, and pitching.

Production is the actual creation of the media content and involves the assembly of audio and visual components. In editing terms, production is the act of creating a source clip (segment or segments of those components) for manipulation in **post-production**, the editing and possible addition of effects portion of the production pipeline.

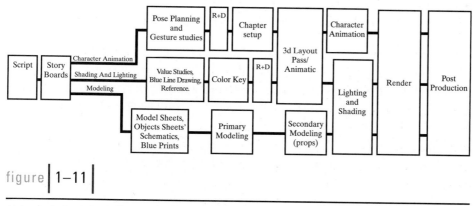

figure | 1–11 |

A standard visual storytelling production pipeline.

So, why do we bother with pre-production? "I just want to jump in and do it! You know, start creating and see where it goes. I don't want to make something that fits into a mold or formula. It will just sound cliché and lack any real art." If creation comes from the heart, from harvested talent, why bother with concrete structures? The fun part is production, actually making the presentation, right?

Wrong. This philosophy ties back to the idea of audience explored earlier in this chapter. If a visual storyteller wants to create work for an audience consisting of himself, then by all means, let the fun flow. However, audiences consisting of people who are not the storyteller place rigid demands on any activity that takes their time and attention.

If you want to build a solid house, you need a solid foundation based on clear blueprints. And since paper is cheaper than film, pre-production is an essential step in the production pipeline. Production is labor intensive, and creating just a minute of visual story requires an enormous amount of work in nearly every media–too much work to have to throw it out if it is not to your liking. So, working out your ideas on paper before you commit them to the screen is an invaluable necessity.

| NOTE |

The real reason for pre-production is that paper is cheaper and faster than film.

Ask yourself how you will avoid making mistakes in your story that cost you precious time. You save the resources. The fastest way to a compelling visual story is to take the time to audition all your story permutations and experiments on paper first. Rewriting a script page can take anywhere from five minutes to an hour, while recreating the media it represents could take you days, weeks, or if you have consumed irreplaceable resources, forever.

figure | 1–12 |

Your time has value; use it wisely.

To illustrate the value of pre-production, consider that in the late 1900s, a major animation studio in California had more than 200 people working on its 2-D animated TV shows. The primary focus of their work involved pre-production and post-production. Only a trivial amount of those 200 people's time was devoted to the awesome endeavor of the production step. That is how important it is to complete thorough pre-production.

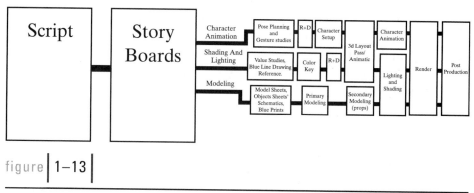

figure | 1–13 |

The primary focus of work involves pre-production.

The following sections touch on the most fundamental and important guidelines for pre-production. These sections give a survey description of the process and are by no means comprehensive. When you are ready to dedicate serious time and energy to the study of screenwriting and storyboarding, you should gather more resources that specifically address formatting and process. This textbook and accompanying DVD provide numerous examples for mapping out a professional-looking presentation.

Pre-production consists of three parts in the process of visual storytelling: brainstorming, concept-formation, and outlining.

Brainstorming

When it comes to generating ideas, people tend to see themselves as falling into one of two categories: those who have ideas pouring out of their heads 24/7 and those who decided long ago that they simply are not "idea people." Now, while it is true that some people can access their thoughts and creativity faster than others, most people are capable of coming up with solid ideas around which a story can be fashioned.

Brainstorming is an excellent way to churn your mind into fresh ideas. While the exact definition varies from one person to the next, it is best to think of **brainstorming** as the random processing of ideas from the brain, in no specific order and with no apparent logic. Because the brain works by associating ideas it knows with those that are new to it, brainstorming gives the storyteller space to jot the widest variety of ideas on paper before the more logical, editorial part of the brain kicks in. You can productively brainstorm in three steps.

Step one: Pick a single word or short phrase that describes the goal you have in mind for your finished product. Write that word or phrase on an 8-1/2 × 11 inch paper or in a pocket-sized notebook. You may also want to doodle, rather than write, to represent your ideas. Some people think primarily in words, others in images; go with your natural inclination.

Step two: Give yourself three minutes to write down as many related words or phrases as you can think of. Do not worry about explaining their association, because this process relies on fast-paced thinking. (If it helps to set a goal of the number of items you would like to generate, then do so.)

Step three: Over the course of the next week, make time daily to sit and write down more abstract thoughts about the topic, based on the things you have heard, seen, or thought of since you last brainstormed on this topic.

| NOTE |

The timeline suggested for brainstorming is a week. It is unlikely that the best possible ideas will be generated in a first sitting.

One option for step three might include carrying the brainstorming paper with you to jot down ideas as they come to you. Another method involves writing for a timeframe that is three minutes longer than the last brainstorming session you had.

At any time in the brainstorming process, you may add to any of your previously generated ideas, because brainstorming is not a linear process, nor is it intended to give you a place for organization. Whatever you do, *do not* erase or cross out anything you have written in the brainstorming process. The weeding out process is a later step.

The purpose of the brainstorming process is to empty your brain of all of the apparent and hidden thoughts associated with a given topic. More importantly, brainstorming diffuses the "I'm-not-a-writer" fear because by simply putting even (especially!) random and crazy ideas on paper, you are writing. And in brainstorming, there is no wrong idea; after all, if you do not know where you are going then any direction will get you there.

| NOTE |

Pick a direction and you are more likely to get somewhere. The only evil in visual storytelling is an empty screen.

Feel free, throughout the brainstorming sessions and process, to talk with people about your topic or to prime your brainstorming session by listening to the radio, watching a related or unrelated visual story, or politely eavesdropping on public conversations. If you keep your synapses firing away, you will find that this process is not only easy and enjoyable but natural–even for people who do not consider themselves "idea people."

Here are some additional tips to help you navigate the brainstorming process.

Writing about People

Observe the people who work, live, and hang out around you. Then, determine the ones you find most interesting. If you are interested in them, odds are pretty good that your passion will easily drive you to write about them. Family dinners and malls are wonderful places to identify eclectic and outstanding personalities.

Writing about Places

Visit stores, parks, offices, coffeehouses, and public events–visit anywhere and everywhere! While you are there, write about the sounds and appearances of the place. (Writing about the taste, feel, and smells of the locale is acceptable, as well, though slightly more difficult in some locations.) Take great note of the types of conversations and people who spend time in these places, as well as mannerisms, modes of speech, and clothes.

Writing about Situations

Find an ideal location and focus on one area. As things happen in that specific space, write them down in great detail, describing the conversations, the interactions between people and between people and objects, people's motions and gestures, and anything else that happens in that particular area.

Concept-Formation and Outlining

Now that you have 1,634 ideas on paper, it is time to begin forming more concrete concepts and outlining the script. Concept-forming is best compared to the sorting of construction materials. Whereas brainstorming shipped the materials (ideas) from the warehouse (brain) to the construction site (paper), concept-forming is the step in which the foreman (the visual storyteller) puts the supplies in easily accessible piles, with like materials near each other. **Concept-forming** requires that the visual storyteller look at all of the brainstorming ideas on paper and begin to sort them by various similarities. There is not a wrong way to do this, and you may find that some ideas are related to several others while a couple only have each other. As you sort your brainstorming ideas, you will begin to notice patterns in your categories. This is helpful to think about, too, as patterns reveal insight into your thinking processes. It will also help you in the next step.

As you move from the brainstorming process through concept-formation, you might be tempted to throw away the brainstorming notes, with an interest in ridding your workspace of the clutter created by that first step. Do not. You may need to refer to those notes at anytime during the pre- or post-production steps.

The next step is outlining. By grouping your brainstormed ideas into similar concepts in the previous step, you have already begun to outline the script. The outlining step of pre-production is similar to the erection of steel girders for a building. The steel girders provide the framework and structure on which you build the building. While this step may feel tedious after brainstorming and concept-formation, it is integral to a successful production. True: very few people will marvel at the placement of the steel girders in the initial steps of construction, but even the most beautiful building in the world would crumble without them.

The same holds for a story with a strong outline. An **outline** is a succinct and organized summary of the key events of a visual story, the ideas of which are taken from the brainstorming and concept-formation steps of pre-production. While audience members usually fail to actively appreciate an outline, they certainly will point fingers if it is missing.

At this point you might think, "Okay, an outline makes my story better, but my idea is a short one, and I really don't think I need to outline it because I'm a visual learner." Wouldn't that be convenient if it were true? Much like preparing for any essay or report, it is easier to create a script from a written outline than from scratch, because the outline reminds the brain of the ideas, the relationship between them, and order thereof–making writing the essay, report, or script quite easy. By breaking a larger task into manageable pieces, the entire pre-production process (and production step, as well) becomes easier as the storyteller is working toward a large goal with a clear plan.

figure | 1–14 |

Breaking down a complex task is a great way to make it feel less daunting.

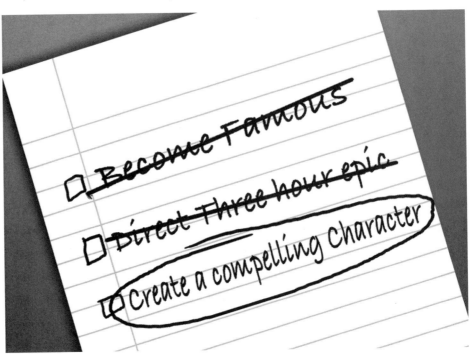

Once again, there are two ways to approach the comprehensive series of tasks necessary for creating a compelling visual story. In the first, and less effective method, the storyteller tries simultaneously to (a) portray an interesting and compelling character who is (b) sincerely challenged by active obstacles (c) in an interesting and believable environment (d) within time and financial budgets (e) while also coordinating the time and schedules of everyone involved. This approach puts too many decisions and responsibilities in front of the visual storytelling production managers and is bound to short-circuit the whole process.

The second and more intelligible line of attack guides the visual storyteller to work through the steps of pre-production from brainstorming to concept-formation and finally to outlining. This allows him to create believable characters, actions, and events because he took the time to imagine, capture, and organize his *best* thoughts. An outline should borrow from the concepts formed after brainstorming to detail all the main events in the visual story: what happens, to whom it happens, and how they feel about it. These will help the character move through his arc. Then, brilliant execution of your idea can wait for production, when you worry about the coloring of the background, camera placement, pacing, and so on.

INTRODUCTION TO SCRIPTS, SHOT LISTS, AND STORYBOARDS

The next step in pre-production is scriptwriting. Once you have a workable script, you will need two more tools, shot lists and storyboards. Just as brainstorming and concept-formation make the outlining step much easier than it otherwise might be, you will find that storyboards assist with cataloguing shot lists.

Scripts

We have established that paper is cheaper than film. It is also commonly accepted that while a picture is worth a thousand words, words are easier and faster to communicate. So scriptwriting follows brainstorming and outlining in the pre-production process. A **script** is a pre-production tool used to commit to paper all things seen or heard during the execution of the visual story. A script is a blueprint for the final visual story; it contains all of the important words to be spoken and images to be shown. A good script contains all the elements necessary to create the production steps that follow it, shot lists and storyboards.

The formatting of a script is a highly stylized process. The visual storyteller must first know who the intended user of the script is before deciding on the nuances of formatting. If the script is to be used by someone else, then strict formatting conventions should be observed. The script should not contain overt descriptions of camera movements or other directorial concerns; it should be focused on *what* the audience sees and hears, not how the audio and visual will be presented. If the script is intended for use by the writer, then it is a useful place to insert notes that will be valuable to the storyteller when he dons the hats of the storyboard artist and director.

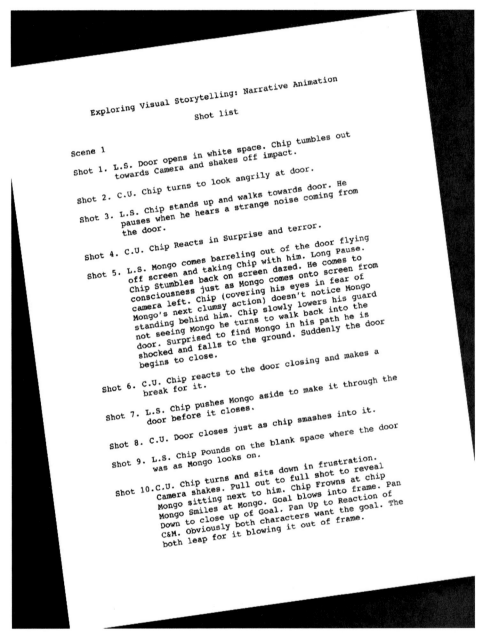

Exploring Visual Storytelling: Narrative Animation

Shot list

Scene 1

Shot 1. L.S. Door opens in white space. Chip tumbles out towards Camera and shakes off impact.

Shot 2. C.U. Chip turns to look angrily at door.

Shot 3. L.S. Chip stands up and walks towards door. He pauses when he hears a strange noise coming from the door.

Shot 4. C.U. Chip Reacts in Surprise and terror.

Shot 5. L.S. Mongo comes barreling out of the door flying off screen and taking Chip with him. Long Pause. Chip Stumbles back on screen dazed. He comes to consciousness just as Mongo comes onto screen from camera left. Chip (covering his eyes in fear of Mongo's next clumsy action) doesn't notice Mongo standing behind him. Chip slowly lowers his guard not seeing Mongo he turns to walk back into the door. Surprised to find Mongo in his path he is shocked and falls to the ground. Suddenly the door begins to close.

Shot 6. C.U. Chip reacts to the door closing and makes a break for it.

Shot 7. L.S. Chip pushes Mongo aside to make it through the door before it closes.

Shot 8. C.U. Door closes just as chip smashes into it.

Shot 9. L.S. Chip Pounds on the blank space where the door was as Mongo looks on.

Shot 10. C.U. Chip turns and sits down in frustration. Camera shakes. Pull out to full shot to reveal Mongo sitting next to him. Chip Frowns at chip Mongo Smiles at Mongo. Goal blows into frame. Pan Down to close up of Goal. Pan Up to Reaction of C&M. Obviously both characters want the goal. The both leap for it blowing it out of frame.

figure | 1–15 |

A properly formatted script page.

Shot Lists

A **shot list** is a pre-production tool used to break down a script into not only a series of actions but also into a clear list of discreet pieces of footage. Each new angle or action intended for the screen should be a new shot on a shot list.

Can't you just take your script and storyboard it? Yes. You can also paint a portrait without the subject in front of you, but it is a lot harder. Just as the creation of a script is easier from an outline, the creation of a storyboard is infinitely easier if done with a shot list. The simple reason for this is rooted in the way that most people think about tasks: the part of the brain that visualizes and is inspired to visual creativity is not the same part of the brain that can map out logistical blocking or make sequential decisions. It takes more time to create a shot list and then storyboard it because the processes require different parts of the brain. The added step is worth it when the storyboarding process begins and the mind is focused on visual execution instead of translation.

Here is how a shot list is generated. Let's say we have a scene that takes place on the porch of a crowded inn, where our hero, Johann the sword-wielding warrior meets with the enemies to hear their demands. A line of action in your script might read, "Johann crosses a crowded room and sits at the long wooden table between two fur-clad hulking warriors." This is a nice, clear image.

When you are ready to translate this action into a shot list, you must answer some important questions. *Where is the camera? Does it move? What is the primary element on screen? Is the focus on Johann or some other element of the shot?* Then, when the visual storyteller storyboards this sequence, a totally different set of questions arise. *What does Johann look like? How are the hulking warriors clothed? What expression rests on the evil men's faces? Does anyone have facial hair?* The shot list helps uncover the logistical details of the shot before diving into the visual realities of the storyboard.

Storyboards

Storyboards are like comic book versions of the story a visual storyteller will recreate in another medium. They are not usually drawn in color, but they do tell a story by presenting a series of still images that represent continuous action. Color should be used when it is integral to understanding the meaning of the storyboard image. For example, green frogs are poisonous, red frogs explode, and blue frogs heal all wounds. The hero is about to grab one of them, and the audience needs to know which one in order to derive meaning. The storyboard artist could simply write the word *red* on the image of the frog, but color is more compelling.

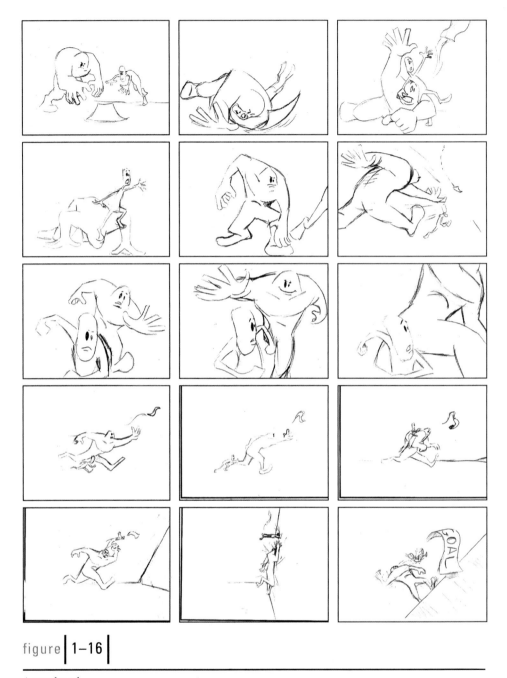

figure | 1–16 |

A storyboard.

To draw effective storyboards, the visual storyteller needs to keep in mind two rules. First, each significant action requires a storyboard panel. If things happen in the story and they do not appear in the storyboard, the artists will not know how to draw them when it is time to create the visual story media and the director will not know how to shoot the live-action footage.

Second, any single panel of your storyboard needs to clearly communicate a single idea, called the primary element. The **primary element** is the action so significant that it required its own storyboard panel in the first place. If the primary element of a panel is Johann preparing to take out his scimitar, then an audience's eye should be drawn to no other portion of the panel than Johann and his sword. The visual storyteller can achieve clarity in his drawings by giving the primary element context (discussed in Chapter 2) and contrast to the surrounding elements and through camera placement (discussed in Chapter 8). In a real production situation or when drawing for one's own use, it is best to think of the boards as "down and dirty." The visual storyteller wants to use the minimum number of lines and shading to convey the meaning of the action. If the artist has to sharpen his pencil half a dozen times while drawing three panels in the storyboard, he may be investing too much detail in his panels.

Once the storyboard is done, it is time to pitch to your peers, who will help you further refine your story.

The Pitch

Pitching is the act of standing in front of a live audience and sharing a passion for the visual story by speaking and directing the audience's attention through the beats of the storyboard. A **story beat** is a singular moment in the story, usually taking the form of an action or reaction. The more energy the visual storyteller puts into the pitch, the easier it is for his peers to assess the strengths and weaknesses of his ideas. No one will like the story more than the visual storyteller, so if he stands in front of a group mumbling apologies for the story while stuffing his hands in his pockets and turning his face to the wall, no one will see the beauty of the creation.

This means that when pitching, the visual storyteller must match the tone of his voice to that of his work. When pitching a story about a happy character, the visual storyteller's voice and energy should be upbeat. If the story centers on a slacker or a vampire, the tone might be altogether different. Either way, the tone needs to match the content of the story.

Another important facet of pitching is to observe the Boy Scout motto: Be Prepared. As the storyteller walks his audience through the storyboard pitch, he must know the sequence of his panels well. To prepare, practice by pitching to a mirror, to siblings, and even to pets. This helps the storyteller work out the kinks before appearing in front of the people whose feedback and guidance he seeks. Their time is valuable, and you can show respect for this by presenting work in its best possible form.

Now, we all enjoy hearing cheerleaders validate our efforts—it fills our ego—but the goal of a pitch is to hone your craft, not collect warm fuzzies. Direct and honest feedback from peers is the only way to grow as a visual storyteller. That does not mean that the storyteller has to make every suggested change, but he does need to listen with an open mind.

| NOTE |

Direct and honest feedback from respected peers is the only way to grow as a visual storyteller.

SUMMARY

Visual storytelling requires a marriage of the artist's unique perspective with the craft of character creation and evolution. To do this well, visual storytellers must use their talents to hone their craft and channel their passions to shape their art. Since everyone has a unique combination of talents and passions, the task of an evolving visual storyteller is to maximize both in order to produce work with the greatest emotional impact.

The purpose of any visual story is to meet the intended audience's expectations by creating an emotional link. This takes place when audience members experience catharsis while watching onscreen characters face an obstacle and reach a significant decision or come to a realization.

In preparing for the production of a visual story, the visual storyteller must engage in committed pre-production work, much like studying a map before a long, complicated road trip. Through careful attention to pre-production, the visual storyteller can make mistakes in the place they cost the least amount of time and effort—on paper rather than on film.

in review

1. What does an audience seek from a visual story?

2. How does the visual storyteller meet the audience's expectations?

3. How does a visual storyteller establish an empathic link with his audience?

4. When should the visual storyteller emphasize contrast?

5. What is the rule of threes?

6. What is pre-production, and why is it important to visual storytelling?

7. What are some of the essential ideas to remember about pitching your story?

exercises

1. List, in order of importance, the value you get out of watching visual stories.

2. List visual stories you have seen that compelled you to relate to the main character(s). What elements of the stories allowed you to feel empathy for the character?

3. List visual stories you dislike. Other than by genre, what do they have in common? What did they do that removed you from the story?

4. Describe a moment in a visual story where the main character had a profound moment of realization or decision that changed his character for the rest of the story. How would that story be different without that moment?

5. Find a compelling visual story and create a script and storyboard (reverse engineer) from one of the scenes.

6. Make a short list of things you are passionate about. Explain why they evoke passion from you. How could you evoke that same passion in others?

7. Think of a visual story you did not like. Now, imagine all the ways that story could have emphasized contrast. Would it have been better?

CHAPTER 2

"Show those things you found about her; those secret things. . . ."

—William Shakespeare (1564–1616)
The Winter's Tale, Act IV, Scene III

objectives

- Define context
- Define the goal of a story
- Compare the value of showing versus telling
- Define the value of brevity
- Explore methods of externalizing intangibles to create context
- Explore how motives and values define character
- Establish how plants and payoffs create context

key terms

context	empathic link	catalyst	intangibles
actions	exposition	dialogue	externalize
goal	showing versus telling	brevity	planting information
emotional experience	conflict	tangible	payoff information

INTRODUCTION TO CONTEXT

Audience members require that events on screen have a clear relevance to either their own personal experiences or to the fictional life of the character(s). Without context, events are nothing more than a series of meaningless activities. *With* context, events are a series of experiences that add meaning to a character's journey and reinforce the narrative's emotional impact. *What happens* on screen (or events) is infinitely less important to the audience than what the event *means* to the characters and *how the event* fits into the rest of the story. Context is the background against which all events take place. It is the framework within which the audience can view the events on screen and derive meaning.

The audience receives new information (context) in two ways; it can be told or shown. The audience is shown information when it sees *action* on screen, it is told information when it hears the characters speak *dialogue*. Context is supplied so that the audience can form an emotional bridge between itself and the events on screen. This connection must happen before the audience will find the visual story compelling.

CONTEXT

Nothing happens in a vacuum—all events take place in relation to all other events, all characters live in relationship to others. The relationship between entities may be loose or it may be integral, but the establishment of the bonds of meaningful relationships between entities and their worlds is known as **context**. Context establishes the relationship between characters and events or objects and people, in order to give **actions** (the images or sounds that an audience perceives on screen) emotional meaning for the audience. Context is essential for the audience to understand the meaning of events. Without knowing how an element (a character, event, or location) relates to all the other elements, events lack meaning; they become random. With context, the simplest of actions can be a powerful emotional experience for the audience.

A character losing his job or being killed is almost meaningless to the audience until it understands the context of the event. The event is just an event. The context of the event is the source of the event's meaning to the character and therefore to the audience. A character losing his job when he needs the money to feed his family can be tragic, a character losing his job moments before he quits can be humorous. The event and character are identical in both situations—a man lost his job—but when the context changes, the meaning of events changes for the audience.

The Goal of the Story

The most important **goal** of a visual story is to create an **emotional experience** for the audience. The audience evaluates the visual story's value based on its ability to deliver an emotionally compelling experience. In order for that emotionally compelling experience to take place, the audience member must observe the onscreen character and identify with some aspect of her actions, words, or general manner. Audience identification with an onscreen character is known as an **empathic link**.

Audience members see characters on screen and perceive the following, "I understand and identify with this character and his choices. Now, when something happens to the character, it happens to me." The empathic link connects the experience of the character to the experience of the audience. Once an audience member identifies with the onscreen character, the viewer undergoes a transformation wherein, at some level, she becomes the onscreen character. This bond is critical for a visual story to be compelling.

Once the audience "becomes" the character, the visual storyteller can confront the character with sincerely challenging obstacles that have meaning for the character; and therefore have meaning for the audience. An audience, confronted with meaningful obstacles, experiences an emotionally evoked response. That response can be curiosity, sadness, anger, joy, or any number of other emotions; the trick is to have a response that is anything other than boredom. The audience's emotional response is evoked by the empathic link with events on screen, but emotions experienced by specific audience members are not always identical, they are still filtered through a set of expectations and personal experiences that the viewer brings to the visual story. So, while a visual storyteller can provide a clear and compelling emotional narrative, she must always be aware that some audience members will bring their own context to the show.

Exposition

Exposition is the stating of facts. Facts are good. Without facts, science would crumble, law would tumble into chaos, and literalists would have nervous breakdowns. But a fact, and therefore, exposition, is not (in and of itself) compelling.

Facts are necessary in the beginning of stories to give the audience context for the actions it sees on screen. These facts lay the foundation of what is normal and real in a visual story world (also known as the status quo) before change enters and forces the character to react.

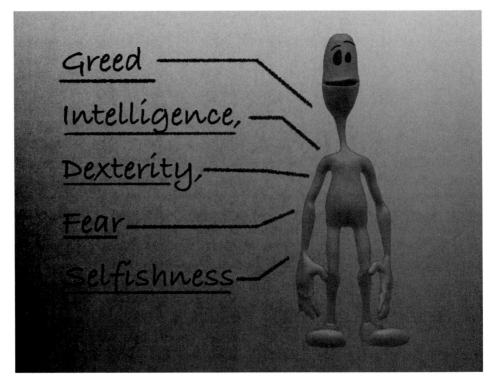

figure | 2–1 |

Facts are not inherently compelling.

figure | 2–2 |

What is normal at the beginning of the story is known as the status quo.

In the beginning of the Chip and Mongo story, both characters tumble through a doorway. The audience can deduce that the two characters came from someplace else because the characters look at their new surrounding with confusion rather than familiarity.

These few beats at the beginning of the story show the audience a new piece of context. Both Chip and Mongo come from a place other than this side of the doorway. Both characters have experienced a disorienting change. After a few quick actions on the part of both Chip and Mongo, the audience sees that Chip is frenetic but selfish while Mongo is kindly but slow. This "normal" set of behaviors will be built up and reinforced throughout the visual story until finally the main character (Chip) is forced to challenge his "normal" behavior and change. In this case his selfishness must be subsumed by selflessness in order to save his new friend, Mongo, from certain death. The moment of change has resonance and meaning for the audience only because it has been so carefully established and reinforced (*shown*) throughout the story. Without that context, Chip saving Mongo might be vaguely interesting to watch, but not meaningful or compelling.

figure |2-3|

Characters need a goal.

All of the information the audience receives in the Chip and Mongo story is visual. Nothing is told in dialogue or narration. The lesson of this example, it is better to show than to tell, is pertinent to all visual storytelling. Exposition is the relating of

figure | 2–4 |

Chip's decision to save Mongo is compelling for the audience because it is a stark change from the behavior established in the status quo.

facts, which can be shown or told. In terms of impact, telling is to showing what a slingshot is to a tank. **Showing versus telling** demonstrates it is better to show than to tell.

So, how does a visual storyteller upgrade her arsenal of information delivery? First, she must firmly understand the purpose of exposition. Exposition, like every other element in a story, serves to facilitate the moments when the audience can share the emotional meaning of events with the empathic character.

Exposition is better seen than heard, however, it is even more compelling when the audience learns new information by seeing it at the same moment a character confronts a significant obstacle. A significant obstacle and realization should coincide. Without the significant obstacle, the realization will feel contrived to the audience. Without the significant realization, overcoming the obstacle will feel meaningless. A character may realize something new or make a decision in light of the obstacle, and these actions will lead to the character either overcoming the obstacle or failing. However the situation resolves, the audience must learn something new and compelling about the character.

| NOTE |

It is better to show than to tell.

| NOTE |

All elements of a visual story should facilitate the moments when the audience can share the emotional meaning of events with the empathic character.

Conflict

Exposition is best revealed during conflict. **Conflict** occurs whenever two forces with mutually exclusive goals interact, such as when characters encounter obstacles. The mutually exclusive goals of two opposing forces act as a **catalyst**, forcing self-discovery and realization to be shared. Conflict provides the heat that pops the kernel of truth. The visual storyteller should provide the audience with characters in conflict whenever new exposition needs to be delivered.

In the beginning of the animation, Chip is propelled into a new world. Then Mongo is introduced. They get used to each other and all is well. Then the goal floats into the scene. Chip wants the goal. Mongo wants the goal too. Both characters cannot have the goal, so their desires are mutually exclusive. We have conflict. The competition between Chip and Mongo for the same resource drives the rest of the story. The conflict forces moments that deliver exposition and motivate the two characters to overcome obstacles; eventually forcing Chip to change his values.

| NOTE |

Exposition is most compelling when the audience learns new information at the same moment a character confronts a significant obstacle.

figure | 2–5 |

Mutually exclusive goals cause conflict.

It is tempting to think of conflict existing in extremes—gun-toting bad guys enslaving innocents in their evil reign of terror. But conflict is a much more versatile tool than that. Conflict is any action or desire that is in opposition to another. It can be as simple as characters bickering over a misunderstood word or as intricate as an intergalactic battle.

An enormous amount of exposition is needed when showing an unfamiliar world to the audience. Intentional and direct delivery of exposition is common and necessary when the time required to deliver the full scope of a story is insufficient or if the content, though necessary for audience understanding, is not compelling enough to warrant screen time.

The visual storyteller can deliver a quick nugget of information that will allow the audience to have a framework for the onscreen events. Then it can zip on to the good bits where characters encounter obstacles and the audience can understand what those obstacles mean to the character. When telling a visual story that takes place (location) in a familiar setting, little exposition is required and the story can get to the interesting conflict (Explored at greater depth in Chapter 4) or obstacles sooner.

Dialogue

It is better to show than tell. However, in the interest of pacing, characters will often deliver exposition to the audience by way of **dialogue** (the words the characters speak). This exposition is often given with the pretext of one character addressing another entity, another character, a diary, or even themselves. The true purpose of the speech is to inform the audience of facts that will allow it to lend meaning and context to the events on screen; in other words, deliver exposition.

figure | 2–6 |

It is better to show than tell.

Audiences need certain information so that they can attach meaning to events, which does not imply that the meaning of events needs to be told to the audience, simply that it has enough information to discover the meaning for itself. This experience of "guided discovery" is one of the values audiences derive from visual stories.

The animation starring Chip and Mongo could have contained dialogue. Chip could have spent screen time talking about his feelings; angst about this strange new world, his frustrations with Mongo, and his driving desire to be the first to get the goal. But this did not serve the story. Dialogue would not have added to the purpose of this visual story; it very well may have robbed the scenes of their emotional punch because seeing the exposition and figuring it out as an audience member (experiencing guided discovery) is more compelling than hearing it.

Still, in all fairness, there is definitely such a thing as great dialogue. Great dialogue does more than deliver exposition; it reveals the hidden motives and values of the character who speaks it, while forcing the other characters to engage in verbal conflict. Great dialogue *implies* more that it **tells,** and it is delivered in a way that reveals interesting or hidden things about the character to the audience.

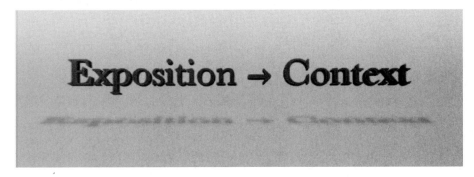

figure | 2–7 |

Ultimately, exposition is the shortest distance between the audience and context.

Ultimately, exposition is the shortest distance between your audience and context. A visual storyteller may have had a grand time designing every diminutive detail of a story world (which is an excellent idea), but that does not mean the audience wants to *hear* every one of the visual storyteller's ideas in excruciating detail. Show an audience your world and the audience cheers; tell them about your world and the audience members who are still awake head for the exit.

Keep in mind the principle of showing versus telling, and always remember, "Fewer words say more." While screenplays serve as a blueprint for your visual story, they are also the "poetry" of the screen; in other words, they use few words to convey great meaning. Anything that can be told to the audience in one sentence instead of five should be.

In a perfect world the visual storyteller would always have the screen time and resources to show the audience everything important to the character. In an ideal world people would eat three balanced meals a day, get plenty of rest and exercise, and call their mothers on a regular basis. Unfortunately for visual storytellers (and their mothers), these things do not always happen. There are always mitigating circumstances that force people to cut corners in order to get everything done in a twenty-four-hour day. So it is with visual storytelling and exposition. Sometimes there just is not room in a story to show a character learning seven foreign languages and training to become an Olympic athlete before becoming a spy; it is just not practical. The information may not be compelling, or it may impede the best pacing for the visual story, so the audience is told.

A novelist can spend lavish amounts of prose time explaining things to her reader. In prose the audience can be told how a character feels. However, a visual storyteller can only tell what will be *shown* or *heard*. Nothing appears on the screen (and therefore in the screenplay) unless it can be seen or heard. This means that no extra words should appear in a script. Characters should say nothing they do not have to. **Brevity**, or conciseness of expression, is your goal in both dialogue and description.

Learning to write brief dialogue takes practice and revision. It requires active listening to other successful visual stories and careful study of compelling examples of great dialogue. Most visual storytelling dialogue is short. Lines are often only a few words long. Normal conversations are not brief or clear; they are filled with vague allusions whose meaning is filled in by body language, repetition, or context outside of the conversation itself. Visual story dialogue is just like visual art; it is representative, not literal. Great dialogue *represents* the ideas discussed; it is not the literal presentation of facts. The *real* way people speak is often inefficient, vague, and tedious.

| NOTE |

Finding ways to show the things that normally remain hidden in people's real lives is the visual storyteller's art, craft, and purpose.

The practice of combing through dialogue to find the heart of meaning and then making that the entirety of the dialogue is the hallmark of an engaging and compelling dialogue writer. No one enjoys rambling. Dialogue often runs long when the writer does not trust the audience to grasp meaning without elaboration.

The process of culling out extra words helps to distill meaning and maximize impact. There are two kinds of moments in visual stories, the moment that delivers a ton of information in a short period of time, and the moment that detracts from the story. Short visual stories labor under this principle even more heavily than long format pieces because the visual storyteller has even less time to build up and deliver an emotional punch.

Tangibles and Intangibles

Audiences prefer being shown new context rather than being told. In visual storytelling anything that can be shown to the audience is considered **tangible**. That means that if it were real it could be touched, but because it is on screen it can only be seen. So, the question then arises, how does a visual storyteller deliver context that involves ideas, thoughts, or feelings that cannot be literally shown? How does the visual storyteller show what cannot be *seen* on screen?

Take a moment and imagine the wind. What does it look like? It is a simple question, but it requires complex answers. People tend to answer the wind question one of two ways, "Wind doesn't look like anything" or "The wind looks like a full sail at sunset or perhaps tumbleweeds bouncing across the desert of the dusty western plains." Both answers are technically correct, but in the visual storytelling sense these definitions of what wind looks like are incomplete.

Wind does not look like anything; we cannot see it or hold it in our hands. Wind is clear and colorless; in fact, technically it does not make a noise Wind is the kind of onscreen element that falls into the category of **intangibles**; an idea, thought, or feeling that does not naturally appear as something a person can hear or see.

figure | 2–8 |

What does wind look like?

"But what about the *howling* of the wind?" you might ask. Howling is audible. What about tumbleweeds and branches moving in the wind? Something holds kites aloft in the park. Those things can all be seen.

Tumbleweeds and kites are visible because they are tangible they are visible in reality and on screen, they are detectable by the five physical senses. What is important to distinguish between is that kites and tumbleweeds are *not* wind. When audiences see a kite or tumbleweed on screen, they are not "seeing" wind. They are seeing the *effect* of wind. The effect of intangibles on the physical world is the way that visual storytellers show intangibles to their audience. The effect of wind blowing through a tight space is a howling noise. A visual storyteller can share this noise with an audience and therefore use audio to imply that wind is present. The effect of wind can be shown as the flapping of a flag or shirt or balloon; the flapping objects can be shown to the audience who then infers that the intangible wind is blowing. Therefore, it is necessary to use tangible objects to give intangible concepts context. A visual storyteller must use a full sail (tangible) to show wind (intangible).

We can apply this same logic to something even less physical—emotions. Emotions do not look or sound like anything. So, how does a visual storyteller show emotions to the audience? The easiest and least effective solution is for the audience to hear about emotions in the form of dialogue (words spoken by characters) or narration.

For example, a character might say, "John, I am both surprised and disappointed that you, my friend of so many years, have decided to betray me." Similarly, a narrator could intone, "John was both surprised and shocked at his old friend's betrayal." Both methods convey the essential meaning of intangible feelings and events quickly and efficiently, but they are not interesting. The audience has no empathic link to this new information and therefore feels no emotional impact.

Audiences have a stronger emotional response to what they see. So, how does a visual storyteller let the audience see intangible emotions? When the audience gets the opportunity to see an emotion, it is empowered to discover meaning for itself. It sees the context and is allowed to experience a guided discovery. In other words the audience gains the satisfaction of having deduced a truth. It experiences a cathartic moment of "Ah-ha!"

So, what do emotions look like? The answer is the same as the example of wind suggests. Intangibles such as emotions "look like" their effect on tangible objects. The audience sees the tangible objects reacting to something unseen and therefore the audience can infer that an intangible is at work. The act of guessing about the exact nature of the intangible offers the audience pleasure. Usually, the tangible object affected by emotions is a character. Visual storytellers translate intangibles into concrete visuals by showing the effect of the intangibles on the tangibles that can be shown. In its simplest terms the intangible concept of happiness can look like a (tangible and viewable) smile (the effect on the character).

| NOTE |

The visual storyteller is responsible for translating intangibles into tangibles for the audience to see.

figure | 2–9 |

Audiences love guided discovery.

So, what does love look like? In the iconographic sense it can look like little red hearts floating out of the character's body; though playful, this cartoon convention will not work in all genre or media. The real answer is that love does not look like anything. The *effect* of love, actions motivated by love, can look like nearly anything, from a tender touch—to murder.

In order to know that it is seeing love, the audience requires context. The visual storyteller needs to **externalize** (make visible) the intangible emotion. Externalization is a set of visuals that either represents the intangible "love" or a series of actions and reactions that show the *effect* of love.

Think about the words and actions people express when they feel the effect of love. Can love look like showing off? Can love look like stumbling speech? Can love look like a great deed or sacrifice? Can love look like a gentle touch? The answer is, of course, yes to all of these examples. Audiences seeing these actions on screen will be able to intuit the fact that one character feels love for another. It cannot be stressed enough that the process of "figuring it out" from the visual clues is a rewarding experience for the audience.

figure | 2–10 |

What does love look like?

The invisible current of emotion and meaning that happens below the literal and mechanical presentation of events gives visual stories their emotional impact. If the visual storyteller offers a story told with only literal visuals, which do not imply any intangibles, the audience will experience all the thrills associated with watching grass grow in real time. Subtext and layers of truth engage audience interest. This is true of great dialogue as well as great visuals.

Events that happen out of context and offer no intangible meaning lack emotional impact. Despite many amateurish visual storytellers' belief to the contrary, this is especially true when characters are fighting for no reason, things are burning for no reason, or people are running really fast for no reason. Actions must reveal intangible ideas or feeling. If the audience suspects that actions have possible meanings in terms of ideas or emotions, it is enthralled. If the audience sees actions that have no context or meaning it becomes lost, disoriented, and bored.

Motives and Values

Characters that make choices based on fundamentally different values (e.g., love, money, faith, loyalty, greed, ambition, or fame) and motives are fundamentally different characters. It is through the demonstration of these values and motives that characters are differentiated, much more than they achieve distinctive qualities through appearance.

Values and motives are the highest level of intangible. A physical intangible such as "the wind" (which is basically an invisible tangible) looks like its effect on tangible objects. Intangible emotions look like their effect on the appearance or actions of the character feeling them. Intangible motives and values are seen on screen when the characters make a clear and visual choice. A new mode of action based on a choice reveals the intangible motives and values of a character.

figure | 2–11 |

Intangibles come in three forms: invisible tangibles, emotions, and motives or values.

The visual storyteller spends a great deal of screen time showing the audience character choices that demonstrate values and motives. In order to command the audience's attention during the screen time necessary to properly demonstrate the choices, the visual storyteller must create tension. Tension is achieved by challenging the character to risk everything in order to make the right choice (more on that in Chapter 4.) The revelation of intangible character motives and values should be shown to the audience, not told. The showing happens when the character faces sincerely challenging obstacles that force her to make a difficult choice.

When a visual storyteller forces a character to make a choice on screen, not only are the character's intangible values revealed to the audience, but also her intangible motives.

For example, Chip is basically a self-involved, greedy guy. Because of his diminutive physical stature, he uses his quick wits to get what he wants, and because of his soft moral code (values), he has no problem acquiring what he wants at the expense of others. His actions and tools include deception and trickery. Chip makes his way in the world by looking out for himself first and foremost. The audience watches as Chip repeatedly decides to do things that advance his own interests at Mongo's expense. Because the purpose of his character's journey is to change his values, he never achieves his goal while using such selfish behavior. The audience watches Chip constantly make selfish decisions, reinforcing the deficient and intangible quality of his character.

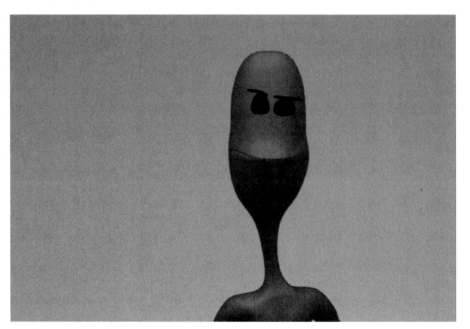

figure | 2–12 |

Greed motivates some characters.

| **NOTE** |

Character is shown through onscreen choices more than by onscreen appearance.

PLANTS AND PAYOFFS

It is usually possible to discreetly provide the audience with the context necessary to derive meaning from events without the audience even realizing it received the information. When the audience sees an event or character action, it retains information about that event or action. When a story is constructed effectively, the events shown to the audience early in the story provide specific pieces of context that give the later events of the story specific meaning. In literature this technique is known as foreshadowing. In visual storytelling the technique of invisibly providing the audience with important context is called **planting information**. When audiences use this planted information to give meaning to events later in the visual story, it is called **payoff information**.

figure | 2–13 |

Planting the information that Chip has extraordinary paper airplane skills.

The trick to planting information effectively is to show it in such a way that it makes complete sense within the scene but is not consciously recognized by the audience as a "plant." Information placed in a scene out of context for the purpose of planting it will only arouse the audience's suspicions and risk disengagement. The planted information must fit within the logic and flow of the scene.

A character who shows proficiency in a skill should deliver extraordinary results under extraordinary circumstances. Therefore, if it is possible for Chip to construct a functional aircraft from wallpaper, it is reasonable to assume that he can fold a monetary size piece of paper into an airplane that will evade flames and strike a small target. The plant of making-the-aircraft pays off when the audience needs to believe that a paper airplane can do the impossible.

figure | 2–14 |

The payoff for Chip's amazing paper airplane skills.

This does not mean that a character must demonstrate ability early in the story in order for the audience to believe the ability genuine. Some of the best stories plant the information that the character is spending a lot of energy to develop an ability that she is only able to finally demonstrate at great personal sacrifice and under the enormous strain of the story's climactic conclusion.

A character who never had the courage to do the right thing may very well take a stand when everything she values is in clear jeopardy. Just like the plant of ability, the visual storyteller telegraphs to the audience that the character is struggling with an issue. The struggle is the plant, the success or failure to display this struggled-for attribute is the payoff.

figure | 2-15 |

The audience believes an extraordinary event because it was set up earlier in the story.

figure | 2-16 |

Events have meaning after the entire context is experienced.

SUMMARY

The goal of a visual story is to create an emotional experience for the audience. If the visual storyteller can elicit an emotional response from the audience, then she has a chance at making it think. In order for thought to happen, an audience member must understand the events she sees on screen. That understanding requires context supplied by the visual storyteller.

Exposition, the process of providing new context for the audience, is best revealed during conflict. Conflict occurs when two forces with mutually exclusive goals interact. Conflict arises when characters encounter obstacles. The mutually exclusive goals of two opposing forces act as a catalyst, forcing self-discovery and realization to be shared. Conflict provides the heat that pops the kernel of truth. When delivering exposition, it is better to show than tell. Telling should only be used as a method of providing the audience with enough context to understand the meaning of events when your characters face obstacles. Once the audience understands the basic meaning of events in the world, it can learn new context by watching. Less is more; keep exposition brief.

A visual storyteller also establishes context by externalizing intangibles so that the audience can attach meaning to the characters, actions, and events it sees on screen. When showing intangibles (things you cannot detect with the five senses) to the audience, the visual storyteller visualizes (externalizes) the intangibles using elements on screen that the audience can see or hear. The more visual the intangible elements are, the more powerful the audience's experience. Planting and payoff information enables the visual storyteller to create expectations (plants) that are either pleasurably fulfilled or delightfully overturned by the payoff. Payoffs are the audience's emotional reward for empathizing with a character as it undergoes its emotional journey.

▶ *in review*

1. What is exposition?

2. Is it better to show or to tell?

3. When should a visual storyteller use exposition?

4. "How does a visual storyteller show intangibles such as the wind, emotion, or values?"

5. How does the revelation of intangibles to the audience create context?

6. Why would a visual storyteller reveal exposition under conflict?

7. How is visual storytelling like poetry?

8. How do characters' choices reveal their values?

▶ *exercises*

1. Draw a short series of panels that show an invisible character moving through a specific location.

2. Write one page of dialogue in which the audience learns that two characters share the same father. Do not use a narrator or any words that literally mean father, parent, or family.

3. List three emotions and draw an image that shows the effect of each emotion.

4. Draw a series of characters demonstrating complex emotions. Go beyond angry, sad, and happy. Try to show subtleties such as melancholy, pensive, and giddy. Show these images to someone else. Does the viewer see the emotion you were trying to show?

5. Watch a mainstream movie DVD with the subtitles on. Track how many words each person's dialogue contains and arrive at an average number. Now compare any dialogue you write with that average number.

6. Write down about five pages worth of a real conversation. Then look for the deepest meaning of the dialogue and boil it down to its essence. Now write the dialogue in its condensed form. Try to express everything that was important in five pages of real-life dialogue in one page.

7. Gather half a dozen jokes and then identify which parts are plants and which parts are payoffs.

CHAPTER **3**

"Show me a hero and I will write you a tragedy."
—F. Scott Fitzgerald (1896–1940)

"What makes us heroic? Confronting simultaneously our supreme suffering and our supreme hope."
—Friedrich Nietzsche (1844–1900)

"Character consists of what you do on the third and fourth tries."
—James A. Michener (1907–1997)

"The Laws of Nature are just, but terrible. There is no weak mercy in them. Cause and consequence are inseparable and inevitable. . . . The fire burns, the water drowns, the air consumes, the earth buries. . . . were [that] Man as unerring in his judgments as Nature."
—Henry Wadsworth Longfellow (1807–1882)
Henry Wadsworth Longfellow (1807–1882), U.S. poet. repr. In Complete Works, vol. 1 (1886). "Table-Talk," Drift-Wood (ed. 1857)

objectives

- Define the main character of a visual story
- Understand the role of a character arc in visual storytelling
- Explore methods of revealing character through universals
- Identify the roles of supporting characters in visual storytelling

key terms

character	perspective character	supporting characters	sidekick
main character			mentor
hero or protagonist	character arc	obstacle characters	
	forced change	antagonist	
	universals		

INTRODUCTION TO CHARACTER

A **character** is a fictitious being who represents a particular perspective or set of experiences in a story. Characters are the conduits through which the audience (as a group) experiences a shared and distinct meaning with the story. A character is traditionally granted a name, yet it need not be human. If an element in a visual story speaks, has feelings about the outcome of events, or participates in the resolution, it is a character.

Character is the cornerstone of compelling visual storytelling. Without a compelling core character for the audience to identify with, the visual story becomes a series of isolated events that have no cumulative meaning. By understanding the tools that create compelling characters, visual storytellers are able to lay the foundations on which exciting events and riveting visuals can be built. Each element of a visual story serves to further illustrate the **main character**, the one who experiences the greatest degree of personal change or who causes the greatest degree of change in his environment during the story. Choice and proper creation of the main character will affect every aspect of a visual story.

figure | 3-1 |

The main character is the source of all obstacles and plot points.

The main character is the most important character in a story and is often the **hero or protagonist**. Some stories feature more that one character prominently; the one who changes the most throughout the story is the main protagonist. Sometimes visual stories are told from the perspective of the main character and sometimes they are not. The visual story experienced by the audience is the main character's journey through the world that forces him to change his perspective or worldview.

Fundamentally, all visual stories are about conflict and change, which is experienced from the perspective of a particular character. That character is known as the **perspective character**, in other words, the character through whose experience the story unfolds. The perspective character is often, but not always, the main character. The visual storyteller's choice of "perspective" character influences the audience's perception of the story's events. Chip and Mongo's story would be completely different if it were told from the perspective of the flying goal.

CHARACTER ARC

The story exists to force a character to fundamentally change either himself or the world around him in order to achieve his goal, something a character wants and has yet to attain. The process of achieving this fundamental change is called the **character arc**. The best character arcs take the character from one worldview to another that is as diametrically opposed to the first worldview as possible; the greater the change to the character or his world, the greater the arc and therefore the more powerful the story. For example, a skeptic filled with rage finds abiding love, a corporate slash-and-burn lawyer becomes an environmentalist, or a small-town farm boy grows up to become emperor of the universe.

In order for a character to attain his goal, he must face and overcome a series of obstacles that require him to change. Characters who fail to change because they cannot overcome their obstacles do not continue though their arc. While a good visual storyteller keeps this in mind, a great visual story must be crafted so that not every obstacle encountered is overcome and not every obstacle results in change. Within those guidelines it is true that some obstacles are overcome because the character sticks to his convictions (refusing to change) but these obstacles do not contribute to the character arc. The audience may experience triumph through the character and revel in his achievement, but unless the adherence to value is a change in the character's behavior, once again, it is *not* part of the arc.

Obstacles that compel change often take the form of other characters and their actions or beliefs. Sometimes obstacles manifest themselves as geographical barriers or societal restraints. Therefore, a visual storyteller is well-served by varying the obstacles that confront the character so that the audience experiences a number of associated emotions and the character's convictions are challenged in a variety of ways.

A confronted character can only overcome obstacles by **forced change**. The forced change happens when the character has no choice but to alter either himself or his world in order to remain in pursuit of his goal. If the character fails to change himself or his world, his goal will be irrevocably lost and the character's life will never achieve the richness and success that the character requires. So, in order to overcome an obstacle, a character must somehow identify his own personal limitations (self-assess) and then choose to adapt to that limitation. In other words, a character must understand one of his faults and change his behavior in order to overcome the obstacle. If an internal change in behavior is not the solution, then he must effect change on his world in order to overcome the obstacle. A character is more likely to try to change his environment first before engaging in painful self-assessment.

How does a visual storyteller create a character who can overcome tremendous obstacles? How does a visual storyteller tell a believable tale of self-sacrifice and painful strength building? How does a visual storyteller convince the audience that it is experiencing something truly heroic and transcendent of self? A good visual storyteller will start by introducing a main character with virtues opposite of the ones he will possess at the end of the visual story. For example, if the goal of the story is to transform a disempowered character into an empowered hero, the most dynamic place to begin that journey is from a place of weakness, flaws, and disadvantage.

A story exists to force change that reveals the character's arc. The story and the arc are anchored by a series of obstacles that dictate the shape of the story and force the character to change. The manner in which a character chooses to overcome his obstacles allows the audience to understand who the character is and how he will evolve by the end of the story.

figure | 3–2 |

Chip must make a decision that leads to internal change.

For example, near the end of the retracting catwalk sequence in the animation, Chip is faced with a decision that challenges his values. In order to overcome his final obstacles, he has to fundamentally change the way he perceives the world and his adherence to selfish values.

At the moment Chip attains the goal he has sought throughout his journey, there is nothing to keep him from walking away with his achievement. Chip has consistently acted out of ruthless selfishness, and now he has the object of his desire. There are no physical barriers to his success, but there is an ethical barrier. Can Chip walk away with the goal and leave Mongo to die? Despite his selfish and greedy actions throughout the story, Chip does possess a spark of humanity that can be fanned into a fire when he catches sight of his companion-rival Mongo in mortal peril. Chip has a choice to make that will reveal to the audience whether he has finally adopted new values or has learned nothing from his journey. Chip must choose between either doing what is expedient or doing what is right. This is the quintessential moment when his character will be revealed. Chip could simply walk out the door and into his happily-ever-after life. When Chip sacrifices his goal (in this case a literal piece of paper with the word GOAL printed on it) in order to save Mongo, he reveals compassion, love, and change to the audience. This final evolution of character has been a silent audience expectation throughout the visual story and by rewarding it, the visual storyteller fulfills the unspoken contract made with the audience at the beginning: "I will lie to you. But trust me, it will be worth it."

REVEALING CHARACTER

A visual storyteller must create an intriguing character whose journey the audience will identify with and whose goals it will wish to see fulfilled. A visual storyteller embarks on a series of steps in order to reveal the character to the audience in a clear and compelling manner. The first step is establishing what is universal about the character for the audience.

Universals

The audience will identify with a character when an element of the character resonates with its own set of life experiences. Some experiences are broad enough for nearly everyone to relate to; they are appropriately called **universals**. Universal experiences tend to be rooted in some kind of struggle to overcome an obstacle. Nearly everyone can point to some struggle in his life. The visual storyteller's challenge is to present characters that are at once unique and specific in their details and universal in their struggles.

| NOTE |

A story unfolds in order to reveal the character's arc. The story and the arc are anchored by a series of obstacles that force the character to change.

figure | 3-3 |

Mongo prefers changing his environment in order to overcome obstacles.

Some people labor under the premise that they are the only people to experience sadness, loneliness, or true love. Visual stories are a wonderful place for the audience to see that the world shares its experiences. Universal struggles allow the audience to identify with the character's feeling, creating a shared intimacy between the audience and the character. No audience member has ever been a hulking blue behemoth, but everyone can relate to Mongo's universal emotions of loss, confusion, frustration, joy, and excitement.

Sometimes a specific character trait can be the connection between the audience and the character. A character with specific idiosyncrasies, flaws, mannerisms, loves, hates, passions, past-times, hobbies, or food fetishes is "human" to the audience and therefore relatable. The key to gifting characters with these nuances is that their foibles be both pronounced and diverse in order to differentiate them from each other while providing points of empathy for the audience. Five characters with the same quirk (they all love to invent gadgets made out of lint) are boring; one singular character overwhelmed with flaws alienates the audience because the character transcends eccentric and becomes irritating.

Peeling the Onion

The trick to balancing the unique qualities with the outrageous ones lies in peeling the onion slowly so that the smell does not drive the audience away. Characters are often just like people in the audience members' lives. When a person first introduces himself with a charming array of personality quirks, he appears human and endearing. When a person presents himself by showing his heart on his sleeve, dumping all of his dirty laundry in front of you, he appears flawed, needy, and desperate.

Therefore, if a character is indeed a social outsider, the full nature of his character must emerge over time. The trick is to allow the audience to fall in love with the character's passions before opening the closet full of skeletons. Small obstacles reveal little pieces of a character's true nature. Only after the audience member and character are bonded can the viewer feel ownership of the character's closet full of skeletons. At this point he will embrace the process of banishing them as if they were his own. The audience's empathic bridge to the character, once established, will create a relationship that can withstand the onerous components of the character's flawed personality. Without that bond, the audience will experience emotional overload and disengage. When the visual storyteller slowly reveals the character to the audience, then the audience experiences the pleasure of discovery.

This universal is analogous to small talk at a party. When person A meets person B, they tend to talk about inconsequential things that reveal very little of their values and provide the other person with the opportunity to get comfortable. This is how people peel the first layer of the onion in real life. Once the comfort is established, conversation usually turns to deeper topics that require the conversation's participants to take small personal risks. This process continues until both parties feel entirely comfortable and share their true thoughts and goals, or one party detects an inconsistency between their worldview and that of the other person and finds a way to disengage. This is how people peel the onion down to its center in real life.

If those same two people met each other for the first time at a party and one of them began the conversation with his deepest thoughts and desires, the conversation would likely be one-sided and short. The person hearing "the center of the onion" first would likely experience discomfort and disengage in exactly the same way an audience does when it sees the character's skeleton closet too soon in a visual story.

It should be noted that a good visual storyteller can follow all these rules and still create a character no audience wants to watch. No one wants to spend leisure time with a jerk. People usually work hard to filter out the jerks in life, so why would they voluntarily spend extra time with one? The question is, how can the visual storyteller excite the audience to form an empathic bond with a character who is, at first, a jerk?

Establishing Universal Empathy

This raises the natural question of why a flawed character is worth an audience's valuable time. After all, the audience needs to make a meaningful connection with a character in order to want to participate in the story. There is no magic to this trick. There are five succinct ways to establish universals to get an audience to tolerate an unattractive character from the beginning of the story. These five universals help forge an empathic link between the audience and the character as it strives to experience the meaning of events in the visual story.

1. Make the character really good at a particular task, skill, or hobby.

2. Subject the character to undeserved suffering.

3. Make the character funny to observe.

4. Show the character displaying kindness to others.

5. Show other characters admiring and respecting him.

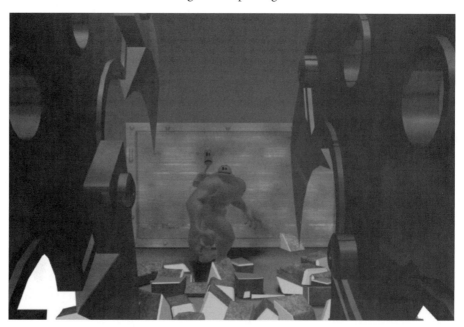

figure | 3-4 |

Characters who experience undeserved suffering evoke both our sympathy and empathy.

So, how do Chip's and Mongo's characters borrow traits from this list? Mongo illustrates universal number one—make the character really good at a particular task, skill, or hobby—by being strong. He is so strong that he can overcome obstacles, such as walls, by demolishing them with his bare hands. Chip is smart; so smart that he can

figure | 3–5 |

Audiences are drawn to characters who make them laugh.

figure | 3–6 |

Audiences trust and feel safe around characters who display kindness to others.

overcome his obstacles simply by imagining surmounting a cliff by peeling wallpaper and folding it into a functional airplane. The audience takes this evidence of prowess as a cue that these characters should be respected for these skills.

Chip illustrates universal number two—subject the character to undeserved suffering—when he is flung out of a door and onto the floor in an unknown world, only to have the bulk of Mongo land atop him. Chip is once again smashed by Mongo's massive body while attempting to navigate the labyrinth. Even with all of his wiles and selfishness, Chip does nothing to deserve Mongo landing on his head. Since this suffering was in no way a result of his actions, which qualifies it as undeserved, the audience takes the cue that this character is due some amount of sympathy. The audience identifies with the pain of the undeserved suffering and forms a stronger empathic link with the character and his struggles.

figure | 3–7 |

Audiences identify with a character's pain.

Chip is nervous and easily startled, which ties in with universal number three: make the character funny to observe. Mongo appears thick-witted and ham-fisted, which entertains the audience with an often rewarded and occasionally thwarted sense of expectation about how each character will deal with new situations.

When a character treats other characters with dignity and respect, exhibiting universal number four—show the character displaying kindness to others—then the audience is likely to find virtue and therefore appeal in his behavior. The audience knows that Mongo is consistently respectful and courteous to Chip despite Chip's disrespectful

figure | 3-8 |

A character facing an obstacle that challenges his weaknesses can often be humorous to observe.

and self-serving behavior. As such, the audience is much more likely to identify with Mongo as a "good guy" than Chip. The lack of kindness on Chip's part makes him less appealing in the story's beginning, in trade for his final moment of thoughtful kindness and sacrifice, conveying magnified meaning at the end of the story.

When one character speaks highly of another character, exhibiting universal number five—show other characters admiring and respecting him—the audience takes it as a cue that the person being discussed has value. Just the same, when an honest character speaks highly of a character that is not in the scene, the audience perceives the statement as truth. In the animation Mongo looks to Chip for guidance on several occasions. Even though that guidance is never delivered, the act of looking to Chip for ideas is a sign to the audience that Mongo has respect for Chip's intellect.

In order for all of these tricks to be effective, the visual story must implement them with sincerity and consistency. One scene of kindness is not enough to establish a character's credibility for the audience. Any of these universal building blocks must be presented at the beginning of a visual story and then echoed throughout for the audience to believe them. Additionally, if character traits are to be challenged at the end of a story, they must continuously and in an escalating manner endure challenge throughout. By using these universals in tandem, it is possible to make any character connect with the audience.

SUPPORTING CHARACTERS EXIST TO FACILITATE THE HERO'S JOURNEY

Supporting characters either assist and encourage the main character to face the obstacles that force him to evolve or provide more challenges along the way to hinder his growth Supporting characters can serve in the following classic capacities. Additionally, any single character may serve in one or more of these capacities throughout the story:

- Perspective character—character from whose point of view the story is told

- Antagonist—obstacle character

- Sidekick—supporting character

- Mentor—supporting character

As mentioned earlier, not all perspective characters are main characters. A perspective character is the character through whose experience the story unfolds. Secondary characters exist to facilitate the main character's journey toward change. When the visual storyteller needs the character to go somewhere or do something that he would never do, it is the secondary character that instigates the new action by motivating the characters through persuasion, trickery, or force.

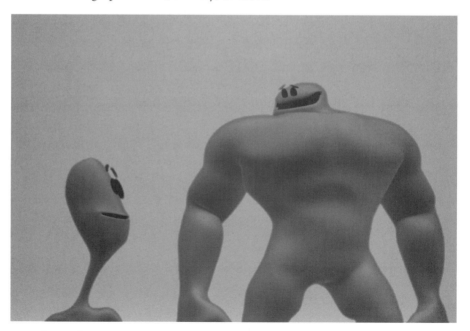

figure | 3–9 |

Supporting characters motivate the actions of the main character.

All characters who *help* the protagonist reach his goal are supporting characters. and all characters who *hinder* the achievement of the goal are **obstacle characters**. Characters can flip-flop their purpose depending on the context of the situation, and in the good stories, they often do.

The character who most actively opposes the hero's (protagonist's) goals is the **antagonist,** also known as the bad guy or villain. This does not translate into the antagonist needing to be a mustache-twiddling sociopath, but depending on the scope of the visual story, the antagonist can be a concerned parent or a snow-capped mountain.

figure | 3-10 |

Antagonists do not need to be mustache-twiddling villains; they simply need to oppose the protagonist's goal(s).

A **sidekick** exists to give voice to the protagonist's deeper and sometimes more difficult-to-share feelings. The sidekick reacts to events the same way the hero would if he had no filter on his own emotions. The sidekick will work outwardly to facilitate the hero's wants, but he will also act as the voice of the hero's conscience, sometimes appearing to work against the hero's goal, but seeking only to challenge the protagonist at a critical juncture, in order to force the protagonist's inner evolution.

figure | 3–11 |

Sidekicks often act as a moral compass for the main character and voice the emotions that the protagonist might otherwise keep hidden.

A common character in many longer narratives is the **mentor**. A mentor takes the form of an older character (usually not a parent) who provides guidance and inspiration as a supporting character. The mentor's role is to challenge the protagonist's status quo and to train him with the necessary skills—both physical and spiritual—to achieve his goal.

SUMMARY

A character is an entity, not necessarily human, that represents a particular perspective or set of experiences (usually someone who receives a name) in the story. Characters are the beings who experience the events in a story and through whom the audience experiences those events.

Fundamentally, all stories are about conflict that causes change. Great visual stories follow a sympathetic character through the character's experience of facing, addressing, and often overcoming obstacles in pursuit of a goal (his arc). A goal is something a character wants and has yet to attain. The pursuit of a goal forces the character arc and is the chief occupation pursued on screen. Supporting characters aid or hinder the main character in his quest.

▶ *in review*

1. What makes a character a main character?

2. What is a character arc?

3. What is a universal trait?

4. What are supporting characters?

5. Do all characters change?

6. Do all protagonists change?

7. What are obstacle characters?

8. What do mentors do?

9. What is another word for the hero character?

10. Which character acts as the hero's conscience?

exercises

1. Pick any feature-length mainstream American film. Document the most compelling internal and external traits of the main character at the beginning of the story versus the end. How did the main character change? Where in the story was he forced to cha___ ___ __ achieve his goals? Write a sentence that describes his arc.

2. Ma__ ___ _____ from any story. Categorize them as obstacle or supporting ch_____ _____ the story?

3. O_____ start and end a story. Now b_____ challenge the character to _____ would need to be in order to _____?

4. _____ does he possess that would _____

5. _____ people would perceive your list _____

6. _____ nimation. Assign possible values _____

CHAPTER 4

"Humankind has understood history as a series of battles because, to this day, it regards conflict as the central facet of life."
—Anton Pavlovich Chekhov (1860–1904)

"We who engage in nonviolent direct action are not the creators of tension. We merely bring to the surface the hidden tension that is already alive."
—Martin Luther King, Jr. (1929–1968)

"War alone brings up to their highest tension all human energies and imposes the stamp of nobility upon the peoples who have the courage to make it."
—Benito Mussolini (1883–1945)

objectives

- Discuss why conflict is essential in a good visual story
- Define tension
- Explore methods of arranging forced action
- Define character lock
- Explore the range of stakes

key terms

conflict	forced action	stakes
tension	character lock	

INTRODUCTION TO CONFLICT

Conflict is one of the few absolutely essential ingredients in all compelling visual stories. It is the catalyst that unearths the buried treasures characters seek to keep hidden. Conflict not only forces change but is the stimulus for expression. It is also the essence of drama. Without conflict, there is no story, for there would be no motivation for change. It does not matter whether audiences seek to avoid conflict in their personal lives; when they sit down in front of the screen, they expect conflict. It is the center of debate, from which truth emerges. Since the exploration of truth is the visual storyteller's primary charge, the presentation of conflict is an essential tool.

CONFLICT

Conflict occurs whenever two forces with mutually exclusive goals meet. The purpose of conflict is to simultaneously engage the audience while forcing characters to confront their own deeper truths. Without conflict, no issues are resolved and no story is compelling for the audience. When a character encounters an obstacle, she must come into conflict with it in order to attain her goal.

figure | 4–1 |

Characters in conflict drive the plot.

Tension

Tension is the emotion experienced by the audience while anticipating conflict. It is invisible energy; the increase or decrease of that energy elicits an emotional response from the viewer. That tension felt by the audience is controlled by the visual storyteller when she manipulates the level of focus on anticipated conflict.

When the audience knows that opposing forces are on a collision course (in other words, conflict is looming) it experiences strong tension. The scale of the tension utterly depends on the type of visual story. The opposing forces massing for conflict can range from a galactic armada to a watchful mother eyeing a cookie jar. The audience, already involved in the story through its empathic link to the character(s), feels the stress, dread, or joy of impending conflict and has a heightened awareness of events.

The opposing forces coming into conflict are often characters, but do not need to be. The threat of a pending storm or the roars of an approaching bear are equally effective methods of establishing tension. Storm and character or bear and character are about to come into conflict; therefore; there is tension.

| NOTE |

Anticipation is the result of expectation. The outcome of the expectation does not need to be positive or negative, merely anticipated. The most compelling experience for the audience takes place when not only the characters expectations are thwarted, but the audience's as well. Be careful; the surprise should be rewarding in its consequence for the visual story.

figure | 4–2 |

The audience watching Mongo await the blades experiences tension.

Creating Believable Tension

A visual storyteller is tasked with introducing elements (desires, wants, needs, obstacles, loves, hates, politics, and ideas) that meet opposing elements in a way that will cause tension and reveal the values of the characters involved. When the audience is aware that two opposing elements are going to meet, it experiences tension.

One of the keys to maintaining tension is that your audience believes that the consequences of the conflict are real. In the world of the visual story, the impact of consequences must be meaningful to the characters. Tension is believable when the audience feels that the motivations behind the tension are believable. Characters that set out to complete heroic deeds for powerful and personal reasons are credible. Characters who undertake Herculean tasks for no discernable reason make the audience edgy. The edginess is the same feeling you would experience when meeting anyone whose motives were questionable. (For more information on motives, refer to Chapter 2.) Once proper motive is established, the audience can appreciate, comprehend, and anticipate the tension of the impending conflict.

Novice visual storytellers often try to recreate the externalities of stories they like without touching on the motives that make the stories compelling. Examples usually include visual stories about ninjas and cowboys who fight for no other reason than that they are ninjas and cowboys. Mobsters, robots, zombies, vampires, samurai, aliens, soldiers, and cops are all character types who are ripe with potential conflict; however, lacking compelling motive, they become nothing more than action figures. These character types can achieve a compelling quality; it is why they are so popular. The visual storyteller must simply take care to establish motive and context before plunging into the gleeful scenes of punching, shooting, and biting.

If the audience questions a character's motives to action, then it is unable to believe in the onscreen tension. When a visual storyteller skillfully presents a character, the values by which the character operates become clear. Genuine tension occurs when a character encounters an obstacle that opposes her values. This tension can only be resolved through a process of conflict with the obstacle.

FORCED ACTION AND CHARACTER LOCK

The conflict created when a character confronts an obstacle forces her to make a choice. She can adapt to the obstacle and change internally, or she can somehow force the obstacle to change. Most characters begin, like most people, by attempting to change the obstacle in the often mistaken belief that external change will be easier than internal growth. But what motivates a character to change? For the answer visual storytellers need look no further than real life.

Consider why people change. People change (primarily) when externally forced—because they absolutely have to, not because it just seems like a good idea. The trick to locking a character into choices that require change is to eliminate any other possible action; in other words, force her. This usually takes the form of the character choosing between the option of change and the loss of everything she holds dear.

figure | 4–3 |

Characters should choose between a forced action and losing everything.

Forced action takes place when a character has no choice but to take a particular action if she wishes to continue to pursue her goals and preserve what she most values. She can no longer stand where she is and she cannot turn back. The only way to move forward is singular; she is experiencing a forced action. This forced action is normally the specific point in the visual story from which the character cannot turn back without suffering life-or-death consequences.

Because change is a fundamental alteration of external surroundings or inner sense of self, people fear it. Change inherently entails risk. Risk motivates people to engage in change only as a last resort, not a first option.

Since people do not like to change, characters that feel real to the audience do not like to change either. This reluctance means that great conflict must be brought to bear if change is to be believed by the audience. Therefore, the visual storyteller's job is to set the stage in such a way that the character is denied any option other than major life

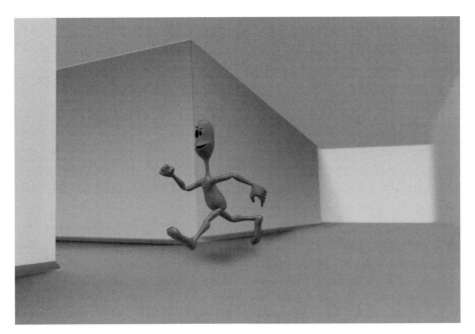

figure | 4–4 |

Sometimes characters change themselves in order to overcome obstacles.

figure | 4–5 |

Sometimes characters change their environment in order to overcome obstacles.

change, because anything less than forced action would be insufficient motive for change. This is especially true when the change is the dramatic kind that fundamentally alters the character's world.

Occasionally, a character can be motivated to change out of sheer desperation; this requires severing all ties to former values. Loss of loved ones, loss of faith, or loss of personal values can create believable pretexts that motivate a character to enter the emotional space that the audience believes is capable of locking her into the events of the story. At some point the character will still require a proactive reason to pursue her goal, rather than the reactive goal of escaping her pain, but as an initial impetus, avoidance is a believable motive that can lock her into a particular course of action.

Once the character's choices are gone, you have created **character lock**. No choices are left to the character if she wishes to continue her quest; and she does. In the story sense, the character is in a maze of choices and the visual storyteller manipulates events (things that happen) so that the character can either move in the direction necessary to complete the story or perish. Regardless of the character's choices, all obstacles result in conflict.

STAKES: FROM A SCALE OF ONE TO TEN

What will a character lose if she fails to emerge from the conflict as the victor? Characters could lose **stakes** if they fail to attain their goals. The more a character stands to lose, the higher the stakes. The higher the stakes, the greater the level of tension associated with the impending conflict. Stakes normally tie into the elements necessary to attain the goal. A character that could lose people or resources associated with attaining her goal is experiencing high stakes. A character that could lose something unrelated to her goal is dealing with low stakes.

So, if Chip were to throw a piece of paper at Mongo in the labyrinth, the stakes would be low. When Chip throws the paper airplane at the red button in the flames and rotating knives sequence, the stakes are huge. Chip just realized that he values Mongo more than he values his goal, and now Mongo is at risk. If Chip fails to throw the paper airplane properly, the thing he values most will be lost. In the first example, the inability to hit his target with the paper has no consequence for Chip; he misses Mongo and life goes on without significant change. In the second example, if Chip misses his target with the paper, he will suffer enormous change. Chip will be trapped alone in a strange world, struggling to reconcile the loss of his best friend.

Depending on your visual story's audience, you will have a maximum level of bad things that can happen. In a children's story the worst possible stakes might be that little Jimmy could lose the friendship of the enchanted pony. In Jimmy's story the

figure | 4–6 |

The goal is often the objective that is at stake in a visual story.

highest possible stakes, on a scale of one to ten, would put the loss of the pony at ten; it is the worst possible thing that Jimmy could experience and the potential loss of his pony should be what is at stake at the climax of the story.

In a story for adults, death is usually the worst possible thing that can happen to a character; in other words, on a scale of one to ten, death is a ten. So, the more often a story can revolve around conflict whose stakes are life and death, the more compelling the story becomes for the audience. Taken a step further, the death of a loved one, the entire human race, or the unraveling of the fabric of reality itself are stakes worthy of an adult story "ten." The trick is to keep in mind that the level of stakes must always revolve around what the loss means to the main character. The biggest events are not necessarily the biggest stakes. Often a character will be more deeply affected by the personal loss of a loved one than the impersonal loss of millions through global disaster.

When visual storytellers determine stakes, they need to imagine what events would cause the most trauma to their main character and then craft the story to lead to the moment when all the worst possible things (to the character) stand to be lost if she fails in her quest.

Stakes are not just about the climax of the story; stakes rise from the beginning. A visual story will build to a moment when the stakes are life and death for the main character. But the audience can better appreciate that moment if the initial stakes of

figure | 4–7 |

Death is the highest stake.

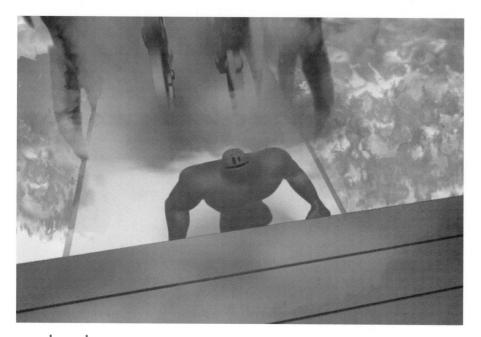

figure | 4–8 |

When great things stand to be lost, choices become compelling.

the story are low and climb like a roller coaster ascending to the highest peak of the ride. Stakes early in a story usually have mild consequences for the main character. But as the stakes increase, she feels their urgency and experiences greater motivation to change internally. Thus the main character is motivated to progress through her character arc.

figure | 4-9 |

Stakes begin low and escalate as the story progresses.

As the story unfolds, new obstacles are layered in, which continuously raise the stakes until they are at the level that is critical for the character. Every time a character overcomes an obstacle, the obstacle is replaced by a new and larger obstacle, which causes higher stakes.

This gradual increase in stakes helps to lock in the audience's attention and provides reasonable transitions for the character's eventual dramatic change. Only under this ramped-up structure will the audience be able to follow the meaning of events and then believe a character's choices when she undergoes significant internal change.

How Does the Visual Storyteller Show that the Character Cares about the Goal?

Stakes focus on the character. A *character* determines the value of the stakes, not the stakes' empirical value in the world. If a story revolves around stakes that are intensely valuable to the character, then the audience feels the character's tension. Conversely,

| NOTE |

Think about your own time management skills. How do you choose when to do the unpleasant things you need to do? People react to stakes in the same manner as characters. When the stakes are high, actions are taken, even unpleasant ones.

events that are meaningful in the audience's world are not necessarily meaningful to the character. If the audience fails to perceive the relevance of the stakes to the character, then the audience will disengage.

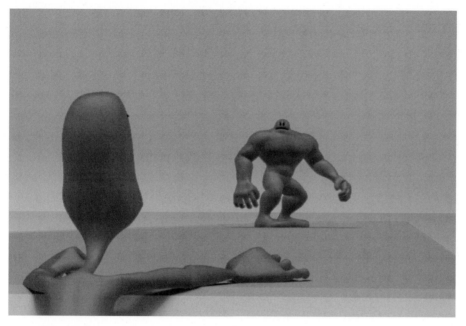

figure | 4–10 |

Events are meaningful to the audience when they are meaningful to the character on screen.

For most of the audience, coming into a huge amount of money would be a big deal; for a character it may not be. For most of the audience, the loss of a parent would be life-altering; a character in a visual story may not hold that value. To most of us, getting our picture in the local newspaper would be mildly amusing and a conversation piece for a few weeks. For a character it might be the difference between a life worth living and one that is not. Stakes are important, not because they may be extreme, but because of the degree to which the character holds them in high esteem. As the saying goes, one man's trash is another man's treasure. Make sure that the stakes revolve around the character's version of treasure.

The visual storyteller shows a character "caring" when the character is in active pursuit of a goal that holds great stake for her. When the audience understands that the loss of the goal would be devastating to her, the audience knows that the goal is something about which the character cares deeply. By allowing the character to put herself in jeopardy to pursue a goal, the visual storyteller shows the audience that she cares.

figure | 4–11 |

Stakes revolve around the characters' values.

Why Does the Audience Derive Meaning from the Stakes?

The visual storyteller's task is to establish context, or *meaning*, for events. The audience needs context to understand the stakes. Audiences are smart; they can intuit, deduce, and guess like nobody's business, but that does not mean that they always want to. Audiences want to be clearly told how to feel about the events in a story. They may disagree with the instruction, but at least audiences know what the visual storyteller wants to convey about her story. People spend much of their day guessing at the meaning of real-life events and actions. Well-told visual stories interpret the intended meaning of actions and events for the audience. By taking away the uncertainty, audience members will feel comfortable enough in their new fantastic environment to take an emotional risk on the visual story.

Audiences care most deeply about the stakes when, as viewers, they are so fully vested in a character that the character's stakes become their own. This is achieved when the visual storyteller has constructed a world of such compelling detail that audience members have mentally and emotionally transformed themselves into the character. Now when a character experiences the tension of goals at stake, so does the audience.

The intensity of stakes is completely rooted in what they mean to the character. The nature of a character's loss ties right back into her stakes. If a character momentarily loses track of her child in a crowded mall, the stakes are real, but low. The audience assumes she will find her child and that consequences to her will be slight. If the

figure | 4–12 |

Audiences want to take risks from the safety of knowing the values on screen.

figure | 4–13 |

Audiences experience tension through the characters on screen.

audience knows that the child is lost and the mother is unsure whether the child is still at the mall, the stakes might appear higher and the audience might feel more tension. Any piece of context that the visual storyteller adds provides the audience with a glimpse of what is at stake for the character and raises the level of the stakes. If the audience was supplied with the additional piece of context that someone is trying to kidnap the lost child, the urgency for the character would escalate and so would the stakes. The audience, knowing that another character is working to actively oppose the main character's goal (of reuniting with her child) will have a deeper appreciation of the stakes.

figure | 4–14 |

The audience cares when the character cares.

Every member of the audience brings her own unique (and often complicated) set of perspectives and experiences to the story. Void of clarity, intention, and guidance, the meanings of stories would be as varied as the audience members themselves. The visual storyteller supplies concrete and specific details about the world she creates and then layers in a series of rewards and punishments as clues to the audience about the meaning of events to the characters. Once events or actions have a consistent meaning for the audience, then it will feel tension when warranted and have an emotional response to the character's struggles.

A piece of classical music without context implies no stakes for a character in a visual story. Once given a context—such as this music always plays when the villain is lurking in the shadows—then the music, itself innocuous or pleasant, takes on a meaning unique to the story. The music now has a context that implies what is at stake for the character.

Audiences care about the world the characters live in *only* because they care about the characters that live there. Once viewers care about the character, events in the story world take on tremendous meaning, but if that step of getting the audience to care about the characters is skipped, no amount of fancy visuals will evoke a truly emotional response from an audience. When done properly, however, the visual storyteller has the opportunity to reach audiences in a way that will resonate with them for the rest of their lives.

SUMMARY

Conflict occurs when two opposing forces or viewpoints actively meet in a way that communicates tension to the audience. Tension is the result of expected conflict. Tension is believable when the audience feels that the motivations behind the tension are believable. These conflicts and tensions exist to force change. People change (primarily) when forced by circumstance. Therefore, the visual storyteller's job is to create the circumstances that lock the character into a dramatic change. Once the character's choices are eliminated, she then experiences a character lock. No choices are left, only forced action.

Stakes are what characters may lose if they fail to attain their goals. Depending on the audience, there will be a maximum level of bad things that can happen in a visual story. The worst thing that could happen in a given situation should be one of the possible outcomes for the main character. If a story revolves around stakes that are intensely valuable to the character, the audience feels the character's tension. If the audience fails to perceive the relevance of the stakes to the character, then the audience disengages. Audiences care about the world the characters live in *only* because they care about the characters in it.

▶ *in review*

1. What is conflict?

2. What is tension?

3. What is motivation?

4. Why do characters need to be forced to change?

5. How does a visual storyteller lock in a character?

6. How does an audience derive meaning from the stakes?

7. Why are stakes important only when based on the character's values?

8. Do stakes change in intensity depending on genre?

exercises

1. Think of a recent conflict in your life. How did it make you feel? What was at stake? How was it resolved? Adapt that same conflict into a scene in a visual story. Can you make it clearer and more compelling?

2. Write a short visual story in which you take a simple character and lock her into a larger-than-life specific course of action by eliminating all options except one.

3. Find three visual stories from three different genres. Compare the maximum stakes in each and decide whether the visual storytellers got as close to "ten" as they possibly could. How else could they have made more at stake for the characters?

4. Ask someone if they ever tried to change a habit. Did it work the first time? Did they eventually succeed? What did it finally take to make them change?

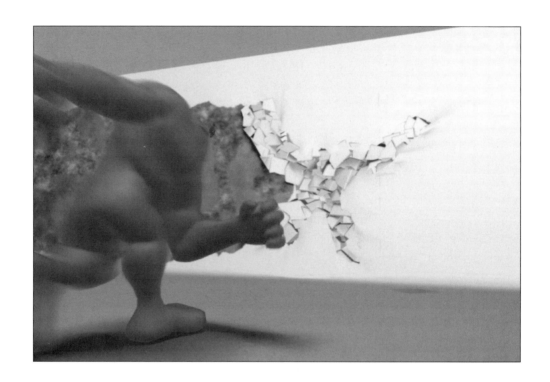

CHAPTER 5

"The beginning sets the rules."
—Mason Cooley (1927–)
U.S. aphorist. City Aphorisms, Eleventh Selection, New York (1993).

"'The plot thickens,' he said, as I entered."
—Sir Arthur Conan Doyle (1859–1930)

". . . A whole is that which has a beginning, a middle, and an end. A beginning is that which does not itself follow anything by causal necessity, but after which something naturally is or comes to be. An end, on the contrary, is that which itself naturally follows some other thing, either by necessity, or as a rule, but has nothing following it. A middle is that which follows something as some other thing follows it. A well constructed plot, therefore, must neither begin nor end at haphazard, but conform to these principles."
—Aristotle (384–322 BC)
Poetics VII

objectives

- Define plot
- Identify what a story is and what it is not
- Examine through line
- Determine what catalyst will motivate a character
- Dynamic tensions
- Explore world-building

key terms

plot	catalyst	status quo	suspension of disbelief
events	scene	climax	
through line	dynamic tension	world-building	sincerity

INTRODUCTION TO PLOT

Plot is a series of events designed to actively challenge the character to change. **Events** are the *things* that happen in a story. Plot is made up of events. Events are made up of actions. Actions are initiated by characters. Therefore, characters drive events, which in turn drive the plot. Character is the source of plot. Plot contains a thread of events running through the story that force the main characters to change themselves or their environment. Events are organized into three acts that, in sequence, (1) introduce the problem, (2) show the character trying to solve the problem, and then (3) show the character dealing with the new reality created by the solution.

Notice the element of three in the organization of events. As you learned in Chapter 1, the rule of threes or the tendency to sequence or quantify elements in threes, occurs across all levels visual storytelling. Audiences respond well to three. An audience feels secure when it (1) is prepared for an event, (2) views the event, and (3) is then able to debrief the event. This beginning, middle, and end structure is effective on all levels of plot; from the microcosm of the scene to the macrocosm of the entire story. The elements that effectively tie all three acts together are known as the through line.

NOTE

Plot exists to facilitate change.

THROUGH LINE

Think of a **through line** as the structure (or main idea) that runs through a visual story. A through line links all plot events and becomes the backbone that holds the story together. Do not confuse through line with theme, which is about the *meaning* derived from the events. Through line, rather, is about the literal events themselves that culminate in a grand confrontation. A through line should be expressible in one sentence.

Every element of a visual story—character, location, plot, theme, and so on—is like a mirror reflecting the through line in a different way. Each element is carefully constructed to specifically show the audience a new facet of the through line. When a visual storyteller understands his story, he will have the ability to succinctly express his story's through line.

The story is about a character that experiences an inciting incident (or catalyst) that causes change and forces the character to deal with a new challenge. In short, you have a character, incident, and change. The ability to summarize a story in this way is critical to its successful expression. Unless you can explain the through line of the visual story in this format, chances are good that you will encounter difficulty in execution and the story will remain unfocused.

figure | 5–1 |

Chip and Mongo must stick with their through line if they are to be the subject of a compelling visual story.

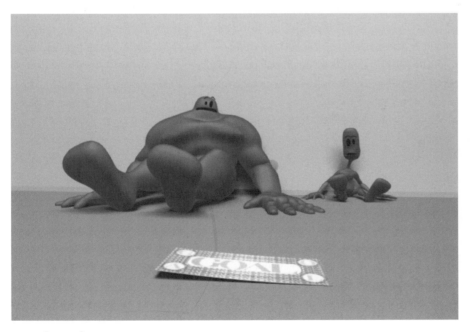

figure | 5–2 |

The goal floating into frame is the inciting incident for Chip and Mongo.

Visual storytellers are responsible for culling out anything in their story that does not contribute to the through line. Any element in a visual story that fails to advance the through line should be removed because it detracts from the impact of the visual story. Without adherence to a through line, the immediacy and emotional impact of the story diminishes allowing the audience to disengage.

Through lines happen when three active C-words mix properly: character, catalyst, and conflict. We will begin with character.

Character

Characters are the entities with whom the audience makes a connection and whose perspectives it follows throughout the story. Good stories flow from character when these three important rules are observed:

1. Location is an externalization of the character's obstacles and is designed to actively challenge the character to change.

2. Plot is a series of events designed to actively challenge the character to change.

3. The character's appearance is an externalization of his intangible inner values.

| NOTE |

Character is the most important storytelling ingredient.

Given these three rules, it follows that character not only matters but is the most important ingredient in a visual story recipe. Everything flows from character, therefore, we spend the beginning portion (act I) of the visual story introducing the character to the audience. The through line is formed by stringing together a series of events that will force the main character to engage in a course of action leading to significant change in himself or his environment. This change is motivated by a catalytic event.

Catalyst

The audience assumes that each character has an imaginary life that exists before the visual story begins. The beginning of a story establishes the nature of that pre-story life so that the audience can appreciate the upcoming change.

In his pre-story life, the main character conducts himself in a normal and regular fashion. The story begins near the end of this homogeneous existence, just before a massive change. That change is a **catalyst**, or an event so profound to the character's existence that his life can never be the same. The catalyst causes the change that locks the character into the plot (the series of events that will actively force the character to change). Now, the character spends a majority of the story pursuing a new set of goals. Once a catalytic event occurs, the old way of doing things, solving problems, earning money, or even breathing, no longer works. His "home" will be irrevocably lost if he does not take action. How does the audience know that the character will rise to the challenge? Because if the character remains inactive, then he will die leaving behind no story.

figure | 5–3 |

There must be a clear catalyst that motivates characters to overcome obstacles.

With no alternatives, a character chooses to heed the call to action. But obstacles stand in the way of his goals, and these obstacles cause conflict.

Conflict

Now that audiences know who the story is about and perceive the looming threat, they are engrossed. Audiences want to see the character struggle (and hopefully triumph) over forces that seek his demise. Those forces thwarting the hero's goals are obstacles and therefore the source of conflict. Recall that whenever two forces meet with opposing goals, there is conflict. Chapter 4 is dedicated to the subject of conflict; here it is explored in terms of through line.

What motivates a character to face conflict in the form of unpleasant and dangerous obstacles? He has no choice. The removal of options removes the power of choice. He is "locked" into his course of action by the new environment caused by the catalytic events. If he refuses to change, he loses everything of value. Conflicts force change and thus motivate progression down the through line.

Audiences eagerly anticipate the moments when characters will confront obstacles.

Characters face unpleasant tasks when they feel that they have no choice.

Once the visual storyteller decides on the fundamental values his character holds and understands the inciting incident that will cause the character to change, he is ready to extrapolate conflicts. Extrapolating the conflicts that arise from change is the process of assembling a compelling through line.

Knowledge of the through line enables the visual storyteller to sculpt a clear, direct, and compelling story. Any character, event, or location can spawn an endless amount of "neat" ideas. A through line helps the visual storyteller to shape those ideas into a compelling visual story.

| **NOTE** |

Extrapolating the conflicts that arise from change is the process of assembling a compelling through line.

figure | 5–6 |

Plot is a list of related events, not story.

PLOT IS NOT STORY

Plot is a simple laundry list of related events; it is not story. Plot is a method of organizing scenes in a visual story, a critical task, but never to be confused with actual story. Story is the impact of events on a character with whom the audience identifies. The story is the sweep of events—in the context of characters' perspective—that shapes the audience's experience. Story is not "Mongo smashes some walls and Chip builds an airplane." Story is "Chip is teamed up with Mongo in pursuit of a goal and along the way learns compassion."

The key to a good plot is that visual storytelling events are organized to sincerely challenge your character. When a visual storyteller fleshes out an idea, he brainstorms all the possible things that could happen to his character that would be interesting, fun, challenging, or compelling to watch. Once that list is complete, the visual storyteller's job (read job as "responsibility") is to cull out ideas that fail to significantly advance the character or story's arc. While it might be super-cool if Mongo were dunked in tangerine-colored paint and forced to fight lizard people to win the hand of Mongette, warrior princess of the scarf-weaving Luddite clan, those events do not contribute to the advancement of either character or story and should be discarded.

Plot is a series of legitimate obstacles that actively challenge the main character. Obstacles can be passive, but active obstacles are more compelling. A bump in the sidewalk, easily avoided, is not a significant obstacle unless the character is an ant. A sidewalk blocked by a herd of stampeding bulls would constitute a legitimate obstacle to a human character's goal of getting down the street. In the animation, plot is what happens as Chip and Mongo attempt to overcome the obstacles of walls, flames, and rotating knives in pursuit of their goal.

Some obstacles are characters. And some characters act as obstacles; sometimes. Mongo acts as an obstacle to Chip achieving the goal through most of the animation, yet he also acts in a helpful manner on more than one occasion. Just as a crowbar that holds doors shut can later be wielded as a useful weapon, characters often act as obstacles in one situation, allies in the next. The more often characters change roles, the more the audience thinks about the characters.

In order to be a compelling part of the plot, an obstacle must be active. For example, parents who oppose their child's goal of attending college can be either passive or active. When they oppose the goal in an active manner, the visual story becomes interesting to watch. For example, Dad may attempt to deter his daughter from moving away by making fun of the name of the school (fairly passive,) or by threatening to withdraw support (a little more active.) He may also visit the campus and make a big scene, slander her name, and tell lies about her to the admissions board. That would be very active because the audience could watch it happen. The verbal obstacle in the first example is certainly daunting over a long period of time, but it is not very interesting to watch, and visual stories do not take place over long periods of time. The father's threat of withdrawing support limits the daughter's options, but does not lock her into a specific course of action. She could borrow money, get any number of jobs, or turn to a life of crime. The obstacle of removed support is only moderately active, and so the variety of ways she could still attain her

figure | 5–7 |

Characters who are allies at one moment can become obstacles in the next.

goal remain fairly wide open. The destruction of credibility in the one place she requires it is very active; she now has to work harder to attain something that was already difficult. Active obstacle characters reveal more interesting things about both the obstacle character and the hero when they collide in conflict.

Always look for ways to make obstacles bigger, stronger, faster, and unpleasant; this will ensure that they remain active. Good obstacles require that the main character do something significant and costly in order to avoid the obstacle—obstacles that can be ignored are ineffective. Remember that the audience needs to believe that events force a character to give up safety for the chance at success.

CHARACTER, LOCATION, AND EVENT

Before constructing a plot, the visual storyteller must establish character, location, and event. These three seeds grow into the through line, which in turn bears the fruit of a plot. Choices about the nature of the character inform the nature of location and event, these two elements serve to facilitate the character's arc, but all three should be considered before moving on to a through line and plot.

The character is the heart of the visual story. It is in service of the character's arc that all other elements of the story exist. Dynamic locations and events are chosen in order to challenge the character to change. The visual story should not just go to someplace (location) "cool" to see "cool" stuff (event) happen. The audience will not respond to locations or events, no matter how gorgeous or interesting, if they are irrelevant to the character's journey. Locations and events that actively challenge the character are cool on their own.

figure | 5–8 |

Establish location for the audience.

SCENE CONSTRUCTION

A **scene** in a visual story is all the action that takes place until there is a significant change in time or location. Many events can take place in the same location at about the same time and still be part of the same scene. Many characters can come and go within the same scene. Obstacles and changes of direction can be limitless, but as soon as the camera jumps to a significantly new place or time, a new scene begins. (Scene is explored again in Chapter 6.)

Good scenes, like good stories, emphasize contrast. If there are two characters on screen, making them both average is not nearly as interesting as making one a giant and the other a jockey. If the last scene occurred on a mountaintop then the next scene will be more compelling if it takes place in the dungeons of a castle. If a character enters a scene happy, then end the scene (in contrast) with the character emotionally devastated. If the scene begins relaxed, consider ending the scene at a frenetic pace. Scenes that emphasize contrast make their purpose, message, and content clear while arresting an audience's attention and creating a feeling of movement.

figure | 5–9 |

Four different locations.

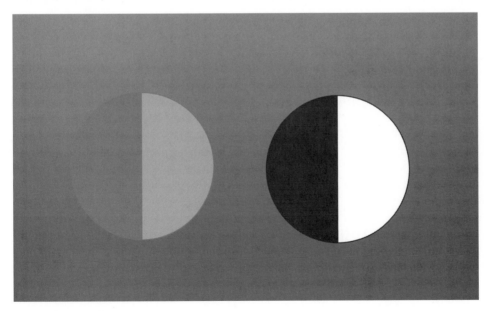

figure | 5–10 |

Always emphasize contrast.

Good stories cover a wide range of elements between beginning and end. These elements or details provide audiences with emotional experiences while simultaneously sharing new information. The new information serves as context in future scenes.

Dynamic tension is the degree to which details of a character, scene, or emotion change from the beginning to the end. Think of scenes and story beats as a roller coaster of opposites; if the audience experiences joy one moment, tragedy is likely to be lurking around the corner. If laughter was the last beat, tears are the most compelling follow-up. Dark is followed by light, rags follow riches. The overall story should be about the journey from one dynamic extreme to another, but there is still plenty of room to show extreme opposites within scenes.

Consider the possibilities of physical, emotional, and mental range for each scene you construct. Any scene that emphasizes contrast becomes more compelling while meaning grows clearer. Well-composed scenes resemble well-composed stories with an overall contrast between the beginning and end. Scenes, like characters, have a goal. The visual storyteller should think, "Okay, this is the scene where Lisa meets Thor, and this is the scene where Thor takes Lisa to Valhalla, and this is the scene where Lisa has a hard time adjusting to life on Mount Olympus." Meeting Thor, going to Valhalla, and feeling like a fish out of water are the goals of each of those scenes. In other words, they were the reason for the scene's creation and should be the ruler against which every action in a scene is measured.

Like a story, each scene has its own through line that ties the scene together. While random or strange things roaming around in a scene might seem appealing, anything that fails to advance the scene toward its goal should be eliminated. This includes planting information seamlessly within the scene for a later payoff.

Since scene contrast is desired, scenes that build to serious confrontation often begin pleasantly. An inciting incident galvanizes the characters in the scene into action and precipitates the collision of opposing goals. When all scenes deliver emotional impact and impart new context, then the visual story has the backbone of an effective plot.

THREE-ACT STRUCTURE

We said at the beginning of the chapter that events are organized into three acts. A three-act structure arranges events in a visual story into three parts; a beginning, middle, and end.

Beginning, or Act I

The beginning of the visual story, known as act I in a three-act structure, establishes what is normal for the character. Act I also introduces the catalyst that will lock the character into specific action toward new goals, which will be pursued in act II.

The audience wants to spend time with the character in the beginning of the story in order to understand how the character exists in his everyday life. This "normal life" is known as the **status quo**.

figure | 5–11 |

The audience must understand what is normal in order to comprehend that there has been a change.

In the beginning of the animation the audience sees Chip and Mongo arrive disoriented but intact in a new world. A general state of confusion and incredulity are their status quo when the audience first joins them.

When the goal floats across their path, it acts as a catalyst, galvanizing them into action and changing the nature of their relationship. They each have a choice—heed the call to adventure (trade their comfort for possible greatness) or lose what they most value. At some point the main character realizes that he is locked into a particular course of action and commits to it. The moment the main character commits to the new course of action—in a way that precludes turning around and going back to the beginning of the story—act I is over. Chip and Mongo's choices propel them directly into the events of act II.

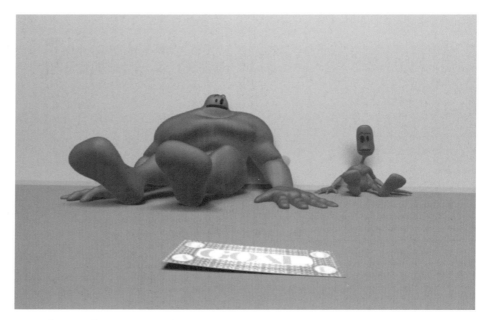

figure | 5-12 |

A catalyst must be introduced to facilitate change.

Middle, or Act II

The middle of the visual story, or act II in a three-act structure, is about the characters undergoing their character arc. Throughout the course of act II, the characters face a series of obstacles. As the characters overcome these obstacles by forcing change in either themselves or their environment, they experience greater obstacles, which raise the stakes of the visual story and increase the tension for the audience. Increased stakes bring larger forces into play, which creates larger challenges, which force greater change. Act II culminates in the climax of the story.

The **climax** is the moment when the stakes of a visual story are as high as they can possibly get; a ten on a scale of one to ten. At the story's climax, the main character (the one who changes the most) has to choose between remaining the same and losing his goal, or undergoing a profound change and attaining it by completing his character arc. Once the main character has decided to change, he must face his final obstacle in order for the visual story to come to a satisfying ending.

The middle of the story is primarily concerned with the protagonist working to overcome the obstacle that threatens everything of value. In Chip's case, the thing of value that stands to be lost is the goal. Act II shows the protagonist trying a variety of methods to overcome the new and larger obstacles (sometimes the antagonist is the

figure | 5-13 |

Compelling visual stories have a low point when all seems lost.

obstacle). The protagonist will meet with varying degrees of incomplete success. All the while the protagonist gains new skills and insights; however the stakes grow simultaneously with corresponding urgency.

In act II, Chip and Mongo's obstacle takes the form of a ledge with the goal perched atop; an obstacle Chip overcomes by fashioning an airplane from available wallpaper and Mongo overcomes by sheer brute force. Chip and Mongo are next faced with the obstacle of the labyrinth, which Chip overcomes by being clever again and Mongo by being strong again. Act II builds to the scene where Chip and Mongo must face death in order to survive the perils of the catwalk of flames and rotating knives. This time, being strong and clever are not enough.

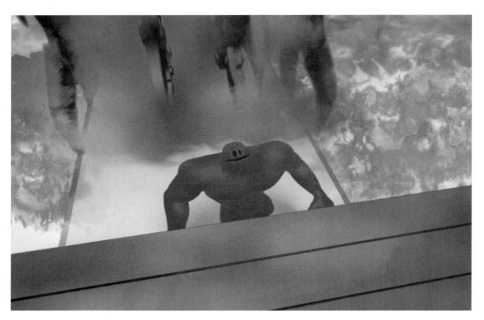

figure | 5–14 |

A character can achieve his goal only after facing life-and-death stakes.

figure | 5–15 |

Goals are not attained on the first try.

figure │ 5–16 │

Stakes escalate as characters move "out of the frying pan and into the fryer."

The middle of the middle should be a point where the scope of the protagonist's goal explodes to include people beyond himself and his immediate loved ones. This time, his proven methods of overcoming obstacles are ineffective and he is forced to change. Chip has to choose Mongo ahead of his personal interests in order to complete his character arc.

figure │ 5–17 │

There must be a clear and tremendously important moment of decision that precipitates resolution.

Eventually, the protagonist must face his greatest weakness—in Chip's case greed—and through adaptation and internal changes master the skills necessary to overcome his final obstacle. Regardless of the success or failure of the protagonist, the end of this showdown is the end of the middle (act II). Once this obstacle has been overcome, the visual story transitions into act III.

End, or Act III

The end of the visual story, or act III in a three-act structure, is basically the new status quo. A new world shaped by the character's arc that changed both him and his world is presented for the audience to appreciate.

The end of the story resembles act I in nearly every way. In act III the visual storyteller shows the audience a new set of normal behaviors and environments established by the protagonist's efforts. The hero, once lacking both internally and externally, has faced his inner and outer demons and emerges victorious. He has a new appreciation of his place in the universe. Act III is where the visual storyteller allows the audience to share in what the events of act II mean for the character's life after the visual story ends. For Chip and Mongo, their struggles and journey in act II have resulted in a new friendship.

WORLD-BUILDING: TRUST AND THE SUSPENSION OF DISBELIEF

Stories are inherently fabricated lies. Audiences go to a visual story knowing they will see a lie, yet they always hope they can trust it. This seeming paradox is only sustainable when the visual storyteller earns the audience's trust through consistency and thoughtful planning.

All audiences come to visual stories with the belief that they are offering up their time or money as half of the following contract:

Any deviation from this contract will infuriate, alienate, and provoke your audience to outrage.

Plot twists delight an audience member when he can look back on the story and say, "Oh, wow! I didn't see that coming, but it makes complete sense now that I think about it. All the pieces were there." Audiences react in an entirely different manner when the twist (the lie) has no foundation in the story they have been watching. Audiences resent unfounded lies and, even more, resent the visual storyteller, "Where did that come from? How can she spring that on us this late in the story? Isn't it convenient that the hero knows how to knit when faced with the dastardly yarn ball creatures from planet Fuzzysweater V. That doesn't even make sense!"

| NOTE |

The visual storyteller's job is to lie to the audience in a way the audience can trust.

"The visual storyteller will lie to me with consistency; in return I will suspend my disbelief. As payment for believing the visual storyteller's lies, I expect my time, patience, and belief to be rewarded with an emotionally satisfying experience."

Brian Arnold

In order to achieve a compelling story, the visual storyteller must achieve a consistent set of rules for his world. These rules must remain constant unless characters take specific actions to change them in the story.

Water does not flow uphill. A visual storyteller may decide that it is high time water did just that, and he is empowered to make that change in the story. What may not happen is that water flows downhill until such time as it is convenient to the story for it to reverse. If water flows uphill, it always flows uphill. If the story is about water changing direction, then so be it, but the altering of any of the basic rules of a visual story is no trivial matter. The magical transformation must be built up and "sold" to the audience. Rules are consistent. If they change, then the change must happen before the audience's eyes so that it feels the change is well founded. Audiences come to a visual story to see change, so do not cheat them of the opportunity to witness a good one. The setting in which the story takes place, or "the world" must obey a consistent set of rules.

An earned change, one struggled for and attained, is satisfying for the audience. An arbitrary change, one that suits the moment, breaks the magic of suspended disbelief and reminds the audience that what it is watching is a lie; and a bad one at that.

Consistency and change lead naturally to the question of **sincerity**, a moment in the visual story where the audience truly believes that the character to whom it has been introduced exhibited a particular set of legitimate skills. Does the audience believe the moment or not? Adequate context must be established to sell the lie.

A sincere moment is not rooted in conflict or the audience's reality. A sincere story moment is one in which the audience truly believes that the character to whom it has been introduced would make the choices she sees. A woman sacrifices her life to save her beloved daughter. Audiences need very little prompting to believe the sincerity of the action; it is a sincere choice to which most of them can relate.

If a greedy industrialist gives away all his money to the homeless and takes up missionary work in Peru, then the audience might require a little ramp-up time on the sincerity angle. The audience would need to see a great deal of justification to believe this sacrifice and change. Without motive, a greedy person's magnanimous actions feel insincere; this forcefully reminds the audience of the lie.

Chip chooses the selfless act of sacrificing his goal in order to save the life of his rival, Mongo. Without context, this moment would have been insincere, within the context of the visual story, the audience can easily identify the reasons for Chip's change of heart and enjoy the moment.

| NOTE |

World-Building is the process of creating a consistent set of rules which serve as the reality in the world created by the visual storyteller.

Audiences need to feel safe in the knowledge that the visual storyteller thought through the story more thoroughly than the audience can in the moment. Audiences want to know that a visual storyteller will reward their trust (**suspension of disbelief**) with a believable world based on consistent logic. This world should allow them to *feel* or *mentally affirm* that something they desperately want to believe possible is true. Conversely, the story may be a cautionary tale, warning the audience to mend its ways. Sometimes, in the interest of pure escapism, an audience simply wants to share the visual storyteller's imagination and see the world through his eyes.

| NOTE |

Any deviation from the audience's implicit expectations of a visual story will result in the audience's alienation.

| NOTE |

Character is what people do when no one is looking. Be sure to include those moments in your story. These are the moments that the audience will believe are sincere.

When characters are sincerely shown overcoming great odds to achieve something of personal value, the audience is allowed to feel that the outcomes it had hoped for were actually possible. This seeing-potential-is-believing-potential phenomenon allows audience members to believe that they can overcome the seemingly insurmountable obstacles in their own lives.

SUMMARY

Plot is a simple laundry list of events; it is not story. Story is the impact of events on a character with whom the audience identifies. The story is the sweep of events in the context and the perspective of the audience's experience. When a visual storyteller understands his story, he will have the ability to succinctly express the story's through line. Visual storytellers are responsible for culling out everything that does not contribute to the through line in order to prevent the audience from disengaging. A visual storyteller further sells the motivation of his character's change by providing a compelling catalyst for change.

Whenever possible, a visual storyteller should emphasize contrast. Good scenes, like good stories, show a wide range of elements from their beginning to their end. Dynamic range should be present within scenes. Locations and events have not only to facilitate the through line, story, and character arc, but they should contrast the previous event or location as much as possible. Each scene has a through line of its own as well as a goal. Once the scene's goal has been attained, the scene is over. The visual storyteller presents the world with a new world which contains a unique system of rules. Over the course of three acts a character undergoes a profound change by facing the obstacles presented by the new world.

▶ *in review*

1. How can a visual storyteller get an audience to believe the story (lie)?

2. What does an event need to be in order to make it part of the plot?

3. Why do stories need a through line?

4. Why does contrast enhance storytelling?

5. Where do stories transition from beginning to middle?

6. Where do stories transition from middle to end?

7. Why is it important to establish "normal" for the character in the beginning of the story?

▶ *exercises*

1. List five significant events in your life. Then break down each event into scenes that show the beginning, middle, and end of the event.

2. Create a list of five characters, locations, or events. Then match each one with buddies, locations, or events that would show the most contrast.

3. Watch a visual story and jot down the plot as you see it unfold. Then write a one-sentence synopsis of the story. Imagine if the facet of the main character that needed to change was different than the one presented. How would the plot need to change in order to properly challenge the character?

objectives

- Understand the difference between 2-D and 3-D space
- Define frame, shot, scene, cut, and beat
- Understand transition, edit, and fade out
- Define sequence, act, and story

key terms

3-D space	cut	edit	story
2-D camera space	scene	fade out	space
time-based media	beat	sequence	
shot	transition	act	

INTRODUCTION TO SPACE AND TIME

Space is *where* things happen on screen, and time is *when* they happen on screen. These simple factors must be considered throughout the visual storytelling process. The visual storyteller's awareness of time and space as tools are crucial to their success. The rest of the terms in this chapter are all constructs used to view time and space so that the medium can be manipulated, explored, and exploited in order to take full advantage of its potential to communicate a compelling visual story. In Chapter 7 and Chapter 8, we will explore more aspects of both 2-D and 3-D space.

Space refers to the dimensions of height, width, and depth. All objects have these three dimensions. A visual storyteller must arrange three-dimensional objects in such a way that when they are translated into a two-dimensional surface (one that has height and width but lacks depth) such as a screen, the audience recognizes those images and can mentally translate them back into three-dimensional objects. In short, you "film" three-dimensional *things* and show them on a two-dimensional surface.

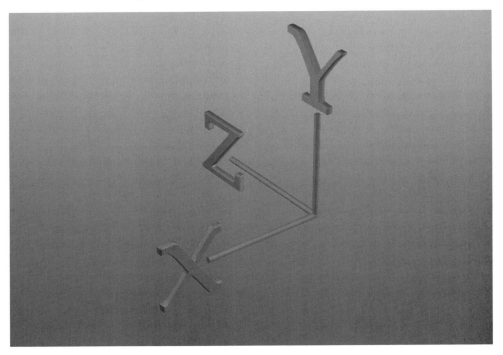

figure | 6–1 |

Visual stories are shown in 3-D space.

Unlike a picture in a magazine, as soon as a *series* of images is shown in rapid succession, the illusion of motion results and the visual story moves into the fourth dimension, **time**. Over time context is built up in the mind of the audience which lends greater meaning to the events on screen.

3-D Space

Three-dimensional space (or **3-D space**) is the normal space of the real world. As we mentioned previously, every object has three dimensions: height, width, and depth. Even the thinnest objects in the world have three dimensions. A person, a planet, and a piece of paper all have three dimensions.

A screen also has three dimensions (height, width, and depth), but the image onscreen is perceived as having only two (height and width). The visual storyteller's job is to translate those images in such a way that the audience will intuitively perceive three dimensions, while clearly communicating the content of the shot.

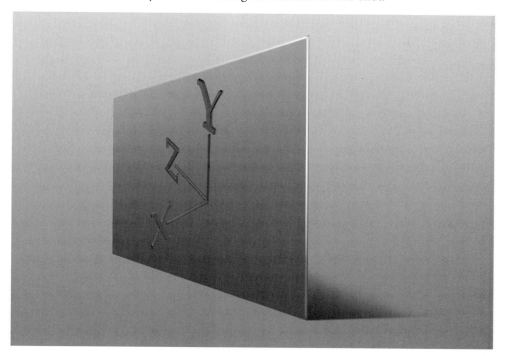

figure | 6–2 |

Two-dimensional space is an artificial construct.

Basically, the trick of composing shots for two-dimensional visual media is to create a two-dimensional image that implies three-dimensional space for the audience. Chapter 7 will explain composition in two-dimensional space in more detail

2-D Camera Space

The visual storyteller paints three-dimensional ideas onto a two-dimensional canvas called **2-D camera space**. Two-dimensional camera space has height and width; therefore the arrangement of the onscreen elements implies depth without actually providing it for the viewer. The visual storyteller manipulates 2-D camera space in order to suggest three dimensions in much the same way a still image creates the illusion of three-dimensional space.

FRAME

A **frame** is a single still image. It is like a visual letter that, in a sequence, makes up the visual words of a story on film. One frame appears exactly like a picture—because it is a picture. The audience sees twenty-four of these picture frames each second while watching a visual story on film. A series of frames shown in rapid succession causes the illusion of continuous movement because the audience is unable to perceive the individual frames. This phenomenon is commonly referred to as *persistence of vision* and works exactly the same way for all electronically delivered media from movies to video games.

Each frame of physical film has sprocket holes down the sides that fit in a projector's sprockets to keep the timing of the film regular. Digital "film" lacks sprocket holes but still tracks individual frames to record progress over time. Digital video runs at thirty frames per second, rather than the twenty-four frames per second of film, but the principle of frames and persistence of vision remains the same.

The presence of more than one frame in a sequence (causing the illusion of movement) makes video, film, animation, and video games **time-based media**. Time-based media forces the audience to view the material over a specific length of time. To see all the single images in an instant would be inscrutable. To view them at unintended speeds would change the audience's experience of the visual story. The effect would be like watching a story in slow motion or at fast-forward speeds. When reading a book, the viewer controls the pace of the story. When viewing a film, the entire audience watches at the same speed. While the film audience could slow down or pause the story in a time-based medium, the meaning of the story would be obscured or altered by the distortion of time. A book suffers no such repercussions when you alter the speed of reading.

figure | 6–3 |

The reader controls the pace of a book.

SHOT

A **shot** is a singular point of view, a kind of visual word, composed of multiple frames. A shot lasts from the moment a camera begins filming until it reaches the next change in place or time. If the camera moves and the audience does not see it move (in other words, the camera is not panning from one spot to another), the camera has **cut**, or "jumped," to the next perspective (an edit was made to the film). The shot ends when the camera jumps. The shot stopped being continuous.

figure | 6–4 |

A cut.

| NOTE |

The primary difference between prose and visual stories is both prose's ability to explain what characters are thinking and visual-based medium's ability to control the pace at which the audience experiences the visual story.

SCENE

A **scene** is composed of multiple shots and is like a visual paragraph. A scene is everything on screen within a given time or place (place equals location).

Like a cut, which is based on a camera jump, scenes are based on a significant jump in time or location. So, if one shot is in the Paleozoic era and the next is in a spaceship, then a new scene has begun because there was a significant change of both time and place. If a series of shots shows a snail crossing a specific leaf for twenty minutes, it is still one scene because there has been no significant change of time or place. If the camera cuts away (moves without the audience seeing it move) to a predatory bird circling high overhead, then a new scene has begun.

figure | 6–5 |

Still one shot.

A scene also positions the characters so that they are visually moving in and out of conflict. A scene, like a shot, ends when the camera moves without the audience watching.

Scenes should begin with an element on screen that establishes location, often referred to as an **establishing shot**. The establishing shot shows the audience where the scene takes place, such as at the base of a cliff, on an airplane, or in a labyrinth. This shot helps concretize the sense of reality and lock in a series of audience expectations about the behavior, obstacles, and resources the characters will encounter. Essentially, an establishing shot establishes context. (See Chapter 2 for more about context.)

BEAT

Unlike frames, shots, and scenes, a beat is not a measurement of physical film but a conceptualization of action over time. A story **beat** is a singular moment in the story usually taking the form of an action or reaction. A beat is usually a moment in which a character clearly and visually appears to realize something or make a decision.

For example, there is a moment on screen when Chip realizes that something is going to follow him through the door. It is a quick moment, but still a beat. Much later, there is a moment when Chip realizes that Mongo is about to be shredded to ribbons. This moment is slightly longer, but still a beat. A beat can also be a moment in which something specific takes place. The moment that Chip takes in order to decide he is going to make a paper airplane is a beat.

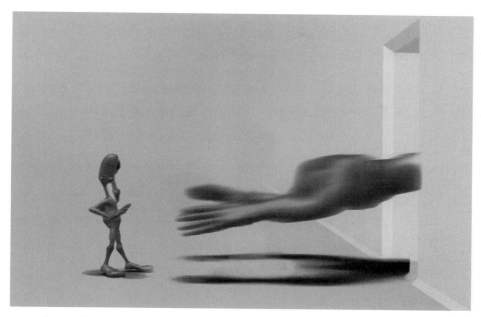

figure | 6–6 |

A beat.

TRANSITIONS AND EDITS

A *jump* in continuity is called a **transition** and serves the purpose of moving the audience to the next important piece of context—without forcing it to experience the real-time journey of the camera moving to the new location in real time. Not every second of the character's virtual existence reveals something new about the character or story, nor is it entertaining or engaging for the audience, therefore, good visual storytellers will omit most of that mundane time from the story.

This omission of real time is an acceptable deception that visual storytellers are licensed (read "required") to wield, and it takes the form of an edit. An **edit** quickly transitions the audience to the next important element. If people were to genuinely experience an edit in real life, they would likely feel traumatized and seek psychiatric attention. The edit only works in time-based media because audiences have been trained to accept and expect this convention.

figure | 6–7 |

A dissolve.

A cut, the most common kind of edit, is basically a transition that happens when one frame follows another, showing scenes that do not take place at relatively the same time or place. So, if frame 100 is a close shot of Chip in the desert and frame 101 is a long shot profiling Chip in the desert (camera jump) then there has been a cut. This kind of transition is instantaneous and usually invisible to the audience's perception. If frame 600 is of Mongo holding the goal in his hand and frame 601 is of Mongo holding that goal a little bit higher, there has been no cut (no camera jump) and therefore no transition.

figure | 6–8 |

A continuous scene.

Most commonly one shot will *cut* to another shot, which means that one moment the audience is watching one thing and the next moment it is looking at something else. Smoother transitions such as fades and dissolves soften the movement from one shot to the next by slowly removing one image while bringing up a new one. These transitions take place over time and are more consciously perceivable to the audience.

In the case of a **fade out**, the first shot fades down from 100 percent visibility on screen to 0 percent visibility while the next shot fades up from 0 percent visibility (a black screen) to 100 percent visibility. A *fade-in* is the same concept as a fade out, but the screen begins with 100 percent visibility and fades up to 100 percent of the first image in the scene. In the case of a cross dissolve, the first shot fades down to 0 percent visibility while the next shot fades up into 100 percent visibility. Unlike either kind of fade, cross dissolves never have a point where the screen is completely dark.

These softer transitions let the audience know that time has passed between the scenes. So, if the audience watches the camera move, the shot continues without transition or edit. If a shot starts with Mongo at the end of a catwalk, then follows him down the catwalk, then records him smashing walls and grabbing Chip, it is one shot. The camera always moved with the audience's knowledge, so there was no edit.

If the camera shows Mongo on the catwalk, then jumps (an edit) to Chip farther behind, and then back to Mongo (another edit), then the audience has experienced three shots because the camera jumped twice. The camera moved without the audience watching it get to its new location.

Describing when the camera moves and when it jumps is one way of describing a shot. It can also be described in terms of the camera's distance from the subject and its length in time. So, distance-wise a long shot occurs when the camera is a "long" way from the subject; a close-up places the camera "close up" to the subject, shortening the distance between the two. Since the camera represents the audience's perspective, the change in distance alters the audience's perception of the image.

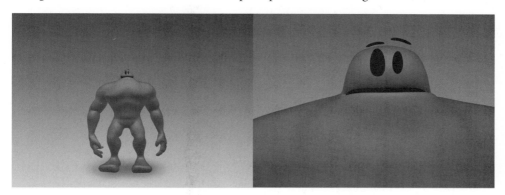

figure | 6–9 |

(1) Mongo long shot and (2) Mongo close up.

Time-wise, a shot is described by the amount of time it takes to be viewed. Given that a foot of physical film contains sixteen frames, and one second of film is twenty-four frames long, an equal amount of film time (one second, for example) can be expressed in three different ways:

Actual time: 1 second

Frames: 24 frames of film or 30 frames of digital video

Feet of film: 1-1/2 feet

Each of these attributes of a shot are also elements of a sequence.

SEQUENCE

A **sequence** is a progressive series of scenes that relate to each other based on their common arc propelling content. A sequence is like a visual chapter. All of the action takes place in one location and in a fairly linear progression of time.

When Chip and Mongo enter the labyrinth, they enter a sequence. Chasing the goal and winding their way though the labyrinth is all part of one sequence that ends when they chase the goal out of the labyrinth and onto the bridge.

figure | 6–10 |

A sequence.

| **NOTE** |

A sequence is like a mini story placed inside the larger story by the visual storyteller.

The element that ties a sequence together is the intent of the visual storyteller to communicate a substory, which fits into the whole story, advancing both the character and plot.

ACT

An **act** is a story structure model composed of multiple scenes; it contains key plot points and encompasses the beginning, middle, *or* end of the story. Unlike a sequence, it serves to track the character though her arc and is not as concerned with the evolution of the plot.

Some stories are structures with three, four, and five acts. For our purposes, *Exploring Visual Storytelling* assumes that stories fall into the three-act structure roughly correlating to beginning, middle, and end. For more detailed explanation of the three-act structure, refer to Chapter 5.

figure | 6–11 |

The three-act structure is the simplest and easiest to use.

STORY

A **story** is a fictional narrative whose goal is to clearly communicate ideas and feelings in an emotionally compelling manner. A story has a beginning, middle, and end (acts), and it follows the journey of a focal character as she encounters and struggles to overcome obstacles, which results in a profound internal or external change in either the character, obstacles, or both.

A story reveals something about the nature of being human, it offers a point of empathy for the audience, and it entertains. Any story failing to do any of these three things, no matter how visually stimulating, will fail to resonate with its audience. It may be the visual storyteller's ambition to make her audience think, but until she has allowed the audience to feel, there is virtually no chance that an audience will engage in detailed thought.

SUMMARY

Space refers to the dimensions of height, width, and depth. Three-dimensional, or 3-D, space is the normal space of the real world. Two-dimensional, or 2-D, camera space is the canvas on which the visual storyteller paints her three-dimensional ideas. It is into space that the visual storyteller pours all of the images and sounds that make up the time-based medium of a visual story.

Different units of time are used to describe parts of a visual story; the smallest is the frame, which appears exactly like a picture. The next larger piece is a shot, which is a singular point of view composed of multiple frames. Bigger still is the scene, composed of multiple shots. A story beat is a singular moment in the story usually taking the form of an action or reaction. A sequence is a progressive series of scenes that relate to each other based on their common arc propelling content. An act is a story structure model comprised of multiple scenes. A story is a fictional narrative whose goal is to clearly communicate ideas and feelings in an emotionally compelling manner. A story has a beginning, middle, and end (acts) and follows the journey of a focal character as she struggles to overcome obstacles, which forces a profound internal or external change in the character, obstacles, or both.

▶ *in review*

1. Which is longer, a frame or a scene?

2. Is a screen two-dimensional or three-dimensional? What about the image on the screen?

3. What are the important elements of a story?

4. How does the editor get from one shot to the next?

5. When does one sequence end and another begin?

6. Review a conversation you had earlier today and isolate conversational "beats."

▶ *exercises*

1. Storyboard one frame of Mongo's action, then board out one shot.

2. Take a picture of two elements. Can you arrange the small element in the foreground to appear large and use the large element in the background to make it look small?

3. Watch any narrative in a time-based media. Note all the transitions. When do the visual storytellers use something besides a cut? What are they communicating to the audience?

4. Create a basic three-act structure for a story, and then exchange it with someone else who has done the same. Now, take someone else's three-act structure and choose one act that you will break down into scenes. Choose one of those scenes and list all the shots, then sketch out some of the frames in one of the shots. Be sure to note transitions (edits).

CHAPTER 7

"Such noble scenes as draw the eye to flow, we now present."
—William Shakespeare (1564–1616)
King Henry the Eighth, Prologue L3\-4

"What is a society without a heroic dimension?"
—Jean Baudrillard (1929–)

objectives

- Explain the purpose and use of composition
- Define line and shape
- Understand how to show the viewer where to look without context
- Understand how to show the viewer how to feel without context

key terms

composition	form	implied line	color
line	spatial relationships	line orientation	light
shape		dominant shape	

INTRODUCTION TO TWO-DIMENSIONAL SPACE

As mentioned in Chapter 6, space refers to the dimensions of height, width, and depth. Three-dimensional, or 3-D, space is the normal space of the real world. Two-dimensional camera space has only height and width, no depth. Visual storytellers compose shots in camera space in a way that implies three dimensions to the audience.

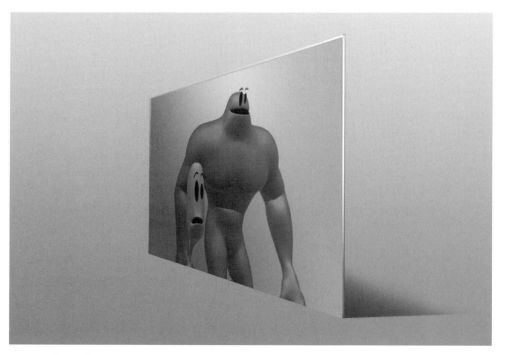

figure | 7-1 |

Two-dimensional images represent 3-D space.

COMPOSITION

Composition is the arrangement of lines and shapes in camera space (the 2-D space on screen). It is the framework on which an image rests. Composition exists to provide the audience with the meaning of an image without having to rely exclusively on context. It is impossible for composition to supply all the information necessary for the audience to derive meaning from a story, yet it is a powerful tool in visual storytelling because it shows the audience where to look (on screen) and how to feel about what it sees.

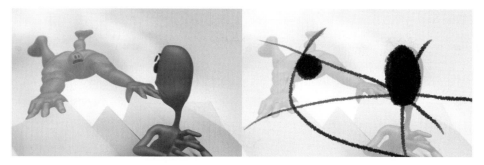

figure | 7–2 |

Composition is the framework of an image.

When the audience sees an image, it immediately has some reaction; this reaction is combined with context to create understanding. The stronger the audience's reaction to the image, the less context it is required to draw upon in order to create understanding. As a tool composition gives the visual storyteller control over the audience's reaction to the images and therefore influence over its understanding.

Images that require little context are easy to understand. The more contexts an image requires for proper interpretation, the harder it is for the audience to understand. If the audience must bring in information or interpret outside information to make sense of an image, its moment of comprehension will be delayed. The longer the delay between viewing and comprehension, the more diffused the emotional impact (of the image) is on the audience. Visual storytellers who use images that require large amounts of context undermine their own best efforts by essentially pulling their strongest emotional punches by delaying understanding.

The audience may need the visual storyteller to add details and specifics of context to give the image a deeper meaning, but not its basic meaning. A well-composed shot delivers its emotional impact instantly. This is achieved through careful composition.

The process of creating an image relies completely on the compositional structure established in the beginning of the process. So, whatever compositional decisions are made when the shot is originally composed must be carried through the entire shot. If the shot is not working, revisit the compositional decisions on which the shot is based using the tools provided in this chapter.

The first step toward understanding composition is to remove context from your consideration of meaning; without context, the mind breaks images down into two categories: lines and shapes.

Line

A **line** is a two-dimensional construct that has length but virtually no depth or width. There are no lines in three-dimensional spaces because in 3-D, lines become forms (explained in the next section). Straight, dotted, and shaded lines all serve as visual pathways to guide the audience's eye from one place in an image to another.

figure | 7–3 |

Each of these are lines.

Shape

A **shape** is a two-dimensional construct, such as a square, triangle, or rectangle. Like a line, a shape has virtually no depth; only length and width.

figure | 7–4 |

Each of these are shapes.

When a shape is considered in three-dimensional spaces it becomes a **form**. The "shape" of a square can be seen as the "form" of a cube. The shape of a circle may become the form of a sphere. The shape of a triangle may become the form of a pyramid. There are no lines and shapes in three-dimensional spaces, only forms. Even a line has a width and depth in genuine three-dimensional spaces.

Spatial Relationships

Composing elements for the screen is ultimately about establishing spatial relationships. **Spatial relationships** refer to an object's location in reference to other objects or to the camera.

figure | 7–5 |

Chip's spatial relationship with the camera is very distant.

The spatial relationship of a 3-D form to the camera is an important factor in creating meaning for the audience. But for purposes of composition, it does not matter what an object's relationship is in three-dimensional space as along as it makes sense in 2-D space. The visual storyteller can alter how forms are viewed in 3-D space manually or with lens length, and as long as the image appears appropriate in 2-D space (the screen view of the finished product) then the discrepancy of the spatial relationships in 3-D spaces becomes irrelevant.

To illustrate, if Chip stands a block away from Mongo and the camera is placed a block farther away, the shot may very well appear as if Chip is standing right in front of Mongo when viewed in 2-D space. The discrepancy between the 3-D reality and the illusion created in 2-D space is irrelevant as long as the image is viewed on a 2-D surface and as long as the shot conveys what the visual storyteller intends it to. If the purpose was to simply show a two-dimensional image with the characters having a certain relationship to each other, then the three-dimensional distance between them is irrelevant to the goal of the shot.

figure | 7-6 |

Chip looks close to Mongo in 2-D space.

SHOWING THE VIEWER WHERE TO LOOK

The screen is often filled with a variety of elements from incidental characters to backgrounds that are necessary for the audience to understand the context of the shot but are not meant to be the focal element in the scene. The visual storyteller guides the audience's eye along a series of important scene elements with well thought-out composition.

Nearly every visual storytelling tool can be viewed as a method of creating contrast. Scene tensions shift from light to dark, characters move from one extreme to another, images pop when they are backed by a contrasting color. The audience notices clear differences and perceives them as important, new information (mentioned briefly in

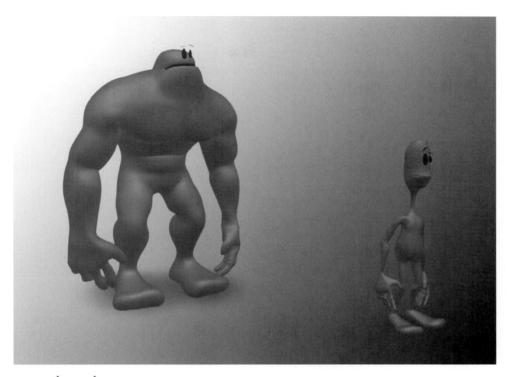

figure | 7–7 |

Chip does not look close to Mongo in 3-D space.

Chapter 1). Visual storytellers apply this knowledge to composing with lines as well. Lines show the audience where to look. Every time the audience sees a line within an image, it sees a visual pathway, guiding it from one place in an image to another.

Line (Showing the Viewer What to See)

A line directs the audience's eye to different areas of an image or from one object to another. An **implied line** is not a literal or unbroken line but rather is constructed in such a way (by repetition of linear elements) as to imply a line. For example, the dashes that divide highway lanes are not an actual line, but through repetition of the dashes (identical elements) in a particular direction, a line is implied. It also helps to keep the motorists' eyes on the road ahead.

Similarly, if an image contains a range of contrast, where one side is of a particular value and the other side is of a different value (black to gray to white or a rainbow) then the contrast between them creates the illusion of a line or implied line. Both implied lines and regular lines are tools a visual storyteller uses to draw the viewer's eye to an element and ultimately show the audience how to feel about it.

Shape (Showing the Viewer What to See)

A visual storyteller wants to draw the viewer's eye to a shape. Lines draw the audience's eye to the shape though their orientation. The shape creates an area of interest at the end of the visual pathways created by the lines. By using composition to create visual pathways, the visual storyteller controls what the audience looks at on screen.

figure | 7–8 |

Lines are the visual storyteller's tool, used to lead the audience's eye to the shape.

SHOWING THE VIEWER HOW TO FEEL

The visual storyteller can also control how the audience feels about what it sees through line orientation. **Line orientation** is the direction or angle of the visual pathway. A line can have basically three different orientations:

- Vertical

- Horizontal

- Diagonal

figure | 7–9 |

Vertical, horizontal, and diagonal line orientations.

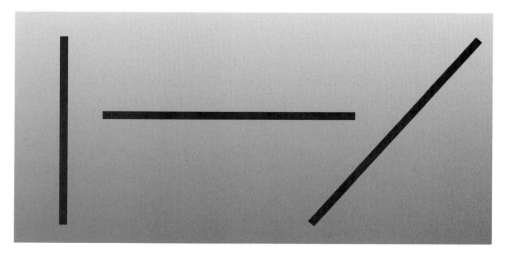

Have you ever noticed how the presence of primarily horizontal lines in a landscape creates a sense of peace? Horizontal lines create a feeling of calm or stability. The opening scene of the animation with Chip and the mysterious doorway has Chip standing on a flat surface that spans the screen. Chip may be disoriented and curious, but at this point, he is still safe.

When Mongo and Chip plod through the endless desert after the paper airplane fiasco and before the labyrinth, the unbroken flat landscape reinforces the idea that the journey will be uneventful and endless. No change is suggested by the flat landscape, only stable monotony.

figure | 7–10 |

The flat unending desert suggests an unbreakable sameness.

In the last sequence with the rotating knives and flames, Chip is flung to safety on a flat surface where the goal lies flat on the ground, motionless and ready for the taking. A glance back at Mongo reveals a character barraged by horizontal action and threat. This contrast is heightened by the line orientation in the scene.

A vertical line creates a sense of strength, power, or boundaries. A skyscraper, giant tree, or any other vertical element in a scene will appear to dominate the composition. When Chip and Mongo encounter the vertical wall with the goal perched on top and out of reach, it feels like a boundary.

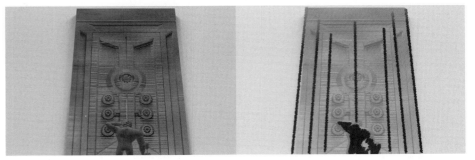

figure | 7–11 |

Vertical lines, like looming doorways, appear as barriers.

Similarly, when Chip and Mongo reach the massive gateway to the labyrinth, the tall, imposing vertical walls provide a sense of boundary. The labyrinth maze itself is a series of vertical boundary-making lines. Finally, when Chip and Mongo struggle across the retracting catwalk in the final sequence, it is a series of vertical walls that prevents their escape.

figure | 7–12 |

The audience knows from earlier scenes that more vertical lines (walls) will pose a significant threat to the characters' escape.

Diagonal lines imply action, instability, or excitement. So, if vertical elements (skyscraper or tree) are tipped diagonally, they suddenly appear to be unstable and ready to take action. In the animation the goal is almost constantly at a diagonal angle when in motion to imply action and excitement. It only rests horizontally when inactive. When Chip and Mongo race through the maze, the camera reorients to show all of the maze walls at an angle (diagonally); this reinforces the sense of action and excitement that are the momentum behind their race.

figure | 7–13 |

Diagonal lines help to convey the sense of urgency in this sequence.

When the retracting catwalk starts pulling Chip toward the walls in the final sequence, the camera changes angle to make the catwalk move diagonal to the camera's perspective.

figure | 7–14 |

The diagonal relationship of the camera lends a greater air of danger to Chip's predicament.

Line (Showing the Viewer How to Feel)

The three types of lines, vertical, horizontal and diagonal, can inform the emotion behind any scene. As demonstrated in the preceding figures, the shots featuring a great number of vertical lines are scenes in which boundaries are visually clear; the shots with horizontal lines feel peaceful and stable. Finally, the shots with a variety of diagonal lines are shots detailing action, danger, movement, and change.

Shape (Showing the Viewer How to Feel)

The placement of shapes has the same affect as the placement of lines in terms of eliciting feeling from the audience. Unlike a line, however, a shape has mass and can affect the audience in a different way. When there are two elements in a shot, their placement informs the audience's feeling about them. For example, when a large form hangs over a character, the audience feels as if the character is in jeopardy.

figure | 7–15 |

By placing the blades higher than the character, they appear more threatening.

When that same large form is placed under the character's feet, it becomes a reassuring foundation and source of stability.

figure | 7–16 |

A large form under a character's feet conveys stability and safety.

The shape that is intimidating or larger than any other onscreen shape is known as the **dominant shape**. This shape need not be larger in real three-dimensional space, but because of its proximity to the camera, it appears larger on the two-dimensional frame of the screen. To the audience, a large mass at the bottom of the frame appears to be stable and therefore safe—just like a line does. That same shape looming at the top of the screen appears threatening because it obscures what the audience assumes should be open sky. A large shape looming over a small shape implies that the smaller shape is about to be overtaken. So, when the large shape of Mongo comes up behind the small shape of Chip, Mongo appears to loom threateningly.

figure | 7–17 |

Mongo, a large looming shape, appears to dominate Chip.

A Word about Color and Light

The non-aesthetic purpose of **color** and **light** is to create contrast. The charge of the visual storyteller is to vigilantly look for opportunities to heighten contrast in all aspects of storytelling. The use of color and light should always be a ready tool for heightening clarity. Contrast in visuals, characters, locations, and story points provide clarity and raise the potential for an audience to experience something compelling. Though *Exploring Visual Storytelling* does not address color and light directly, the goals achieved with color and light are clearly illustrated in the previous sections dedicated to line and shape.

SUMMARY

Composition is the arrangement of lines and shapes in camera space (the two-dimensional space on a screen) and the framework on which an image rests. A well-composed shot delivers its emotional impact instantly. The process of creating an image relies completely on the compositional structure established in the beginning of the process, so a good visual storyteller will plan carefully.

A line is a two-dimensional construct that has length but virtually no depth or width. There are no lines in three-dimensional spaces, where lines become forms. A shape is a two-dimensional construct, such as a square, triangle, or rectangle; like a line it has virtually no depth, only length and width. A shape becomes a form in three-dimensional spaces. Spatial relationships refer to the object's location in reference to another object (or to the camera). The visual storyteller guides the audience's eye to the primary element in each scene with composition.

A line directs the audience's eye to different areas of the image; it is a visual pathway from one object to another. Lines and shapes (in the same manner as color and light) also create contrast to draw the viewer's eye to the element intended by the visual storyteller. The visual storyteller can control how the audience feels about what it sees through line orientation. Line orientation is the direction or angle of the visual pathway. A vertical line creates a sense of strength, power, and boundaries. Horizontal lines create the feeling of peace and calm. Diagonal lines imply action, instability, and excitement. Light and color are always available to help emphasize contrast in a composition.

► *in review*

1. Why would you want to heighten contrast?

2. What is composition?

3. Why should images require little context to derive meaning?

4. Does the audience or visual storyteller provide the context for an image's "deeper meaning"? Why?

5. Why are there no lines in three-dimensional spaces?

6. What do the three types of line orientation imply in a shot?

exercises

1. Take a camera and arrange three objects in a row, with the second farther from the camera than the first and the third farther from the camera than the second. Can you arrange them in such a way as to make the farthest one appear to interact with the closest object in the final photo?

2. Gather fifteen small objects—balls, toy soldiers, paper clips, whatever is handy. Then, compose a shot wherein you decide on one object as the focus. Take a picture and share your composition with others. Did they perceive the object you selected as the primary element?

3. Watch five minutes of a visual story. Create a shot list in which the use of lines is explained in terms of their effect on the viewer.

CHAPTER 8

"Any great work of art . . . revives and readapts time and space, and the measure of its success is the extent to which it makes you an inhabitant of that world—the extent to which it invites you in and lets you breathe its strange, special air."

—Leonard Bernstein (1918–1990)

objectives

- Demonstrate staging concepts necessary for clear communication in three-dimensional space
- Explore camera distance and placement in relation to the subject
- Define the types of camera shots and their purposes
- Define the types of camera angles and their purposes
- Define the 180-degree rule

key terms

staging	full shot	camera placement	down-angle shot
shape	medium shot	camera angle	line of engagement
camera distance	close-up	straight-on shot	180-degree rule
depth	extreme close-up	up-angle shot	
long shot			

INTRODUCTION TO THREE-DIMENSIONAL SPACE

All activities in the real world take place in 3-D space. Audiences expect a visual story to replicate that environment. In order to do so, the visual storyteller must understand the translation process between 2-D and 3-D space. In much the same way that writing and visual arts are representational rather that literal, with careful consideration of the translation process, the visual storyteller can manipulate 3-D space to simulate a new reality.

STAGING SINGLE SHOTS

Staging is the arranging of three-dimensional forms to create an effective two-dimensional composition, in other words, the presentation of any element in such a way that the meaning of that element is completely clear to the audience. If the visual storyteller creates a shot to show that Chip is scared, the shot should be staged so that, above all else, "Chip is scared" is the clearest message communicated by the shot.

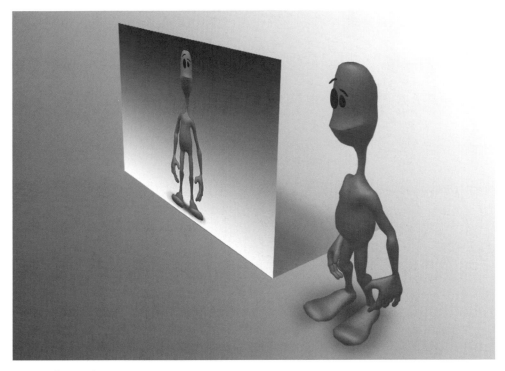

figure | 8–1 |

Staging 2-D versus 3-D image.

Most staging involves the arrangement of shapes. A **shape** (explained in more detail in Chapter 7) is a two-dimensional element that has relatively equal proportion in height and width (as opposed to a line). All of staging is encompassed in the arrangement of lines and shapes.

Three-dimensional space creates complex challenges for staging. While it is true that there is no three-dimensional space in visual storytelling, two-dimensional images create the illusion of depth and the presence of 3-D space in the mind of the audience. This makes depth an incredibly important tool for the visual storyteller. In fact, the element that defines 3-D space is depth.

Staging also involves deciding which camera distance and angle illustrate the primary element of a shot with the strongest emotional impact. The meaning of any element changes with the distance and angle of the camera.

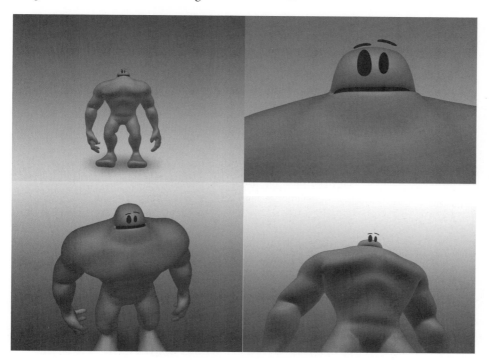

figure | 8–2 |

The staging of the shot changes as camera distance and angle change.

CAMERA DISTANCE

The distance of the camera from a 3-D form influences the audience's perception of the form. Forms and actions change meaning for the audience based on the distance between the audience (camera) and the form. By manipulating **camera distance**, the distance of the camera to the shape, the visual storyteller tells the audience how to *feel* about the images on the screen Camera positioning can alter the feeling of the shot from comedy to tragedy, relaxed to tense, intimate to isolated, uncomfortable to familiar.

Depth is the ability for an element to have distance from the camera; this distance is what controls the size of the object in the 2-D frame. An object close to the camera in three-dimensional space appears large on the two-dimensional image captured by the camera; an object farther away in three-dimensional space appears smaller on the two-dimensional image. Depth is described in a series of standardized shots: long, full, medium, close-up, and extreme close-up.

Long Shot

A **long shot** is designed to show the character in relationship to her surroundings and involves the camera being "far" from the subject. It allows the audience to see the subject's environment very well.

figure | 8–3 |

A long shot of Chip and Mongo establishes them in relationship to the forms around them.

A long shot is often used to establish the location of a character, scene, or event. A camera placed far from a shape shows the shape in the context of its surroundings. This context provides the audience with additional information. This additional information is often critical for preparing the audience to derive meaning from the events it is about to witness.

Long shots are also effective in communicating the enormity of an event or location. By increasing the amount of information taken in by the camera, smaller details are lost, but the larger scope of events and setting becomes clear. A long shot of the desert implies to the audience the sprawling nature of the big open space. A long shot of a spaceship communicates the vastness of space. A long shot of a castaway on a raft in the middle of the ocean communicates the enormity of the ocean and the isolation of the character. A long shot of a character lost in the crowd reinforces the sense of crowd. Long shots are best for communicating grand and epic qualities, or the character's insignificant place within the grand scheme.

Full Shot

A **full shot** reveals a character's entire body and is designed to show a character's actions.

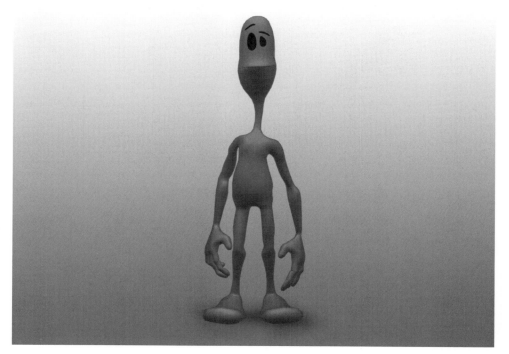

figure | 8–4 |

A full shot of Chip.

By placing the camera far enough from the character to capture her entire body—arms, legs, torso and head—the audience can assess the character's general shape. The camera is not close enough to reveal minute facial details but is closer than a long shot, and the audience can perceive specific details about the character's species, race, dress, hairstyle, physique, and mannerisms.

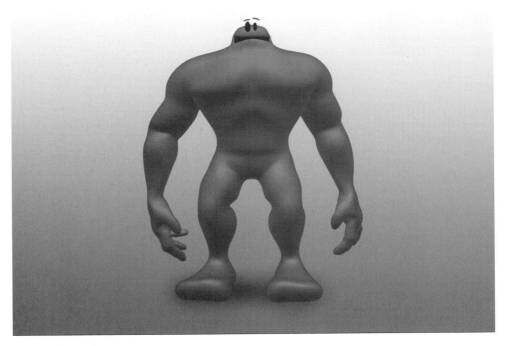

figure | 8–5 |

A full shot of Mongo.

While a full shot will not reveal tiny details, it will offer the audience the opportunity to distinguish one clearly defined character from another.

Medium Shot

A **medium shot** shows the character's upper body or portion of the character's body from the waist up. It is designed to show more subtle action that a full shot, which reveals the entire character. The placement or movement of a character's feet may not be critical information for the audience, while a hand or facial gesture may be. The proximity of the camera to the subject allows for a medium level of detail and a medium level of background information.

figure | 8–6 |

A medium shot of Chip.

Close-Up Shot

A **close-up** shows how a character feels about a situation and usually only includes the emotive part of the body, from the shoulders up. Minimal background information and context is provided in a close-up, which usually lacks clarity of resolution. Instead, a close-up focuses in on a specific action.

The camera typically comes in close to a face (a close-up) to capture an expression that reveals how a character feels about a specific event or new piece of information. The audience wants to know how a character feels, and the close-up is the most direct way to assess a character's emotions. A close-up is equally effective in delivering expositional information by drawing the audience's attention to a specific action, such as a hand holding a gun, pressing a button, clenching in anger, or offering an object.

Similarly, the close-up will fill the entire screen with the shape that is most critical to the meaning of the story's beat, such as a stop sign, a footprint, or a clock. This forces the audience to consider a new piece of context.

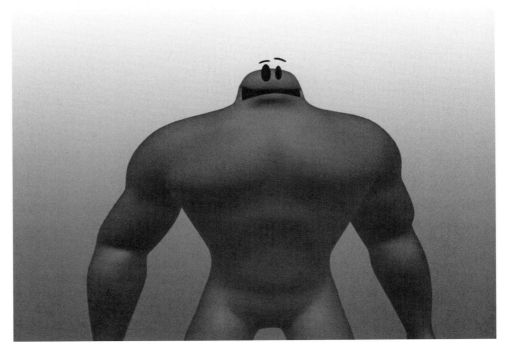

figure | 8–7 |

A medium shot of Mongo.

Extreme Close-Up Shot

An **extreme close-up** shows detailed action or emotion; it usually includes a story detail too small to be captured by a longer shot, yet too important to be missed for the sake of the story. An extreme close-up might be a character's face or foot; it might fill the screen with a part of the shape—an eye, a fingernail, or the sweep of the second hand on a clock.

The extreme close-up can reinforce tension by forcing the audience's perspective into an intimate realm with the object. By drawing the audience in close to the experience, highly detailed and specific information can be conveyed. The cost of the extreme close-up is that all context and perspective are lost in that moment and must be properly supported by previous and following shots. This tool can be wielded by the visual storyteller to cause the audience tension because it is blinded to the larger picture and potential threat in the scene.

figure | 8–8 |

A close-up of Chip.

figure | 8–9 |

A close-up of Mongo.

figure | 8–10 |

An extreme close-up of Chip's eye.

CAMERA PLACEMENT

Distance from the camera is not the only thing that makes 3-D space so complex. Each shot is part of a larger scene that consists of characters, locations, and events. Recall that the process of arranging three-dimensional elements in a scene to create effective composition is called staging. (See the section on composition in Chapter 7.) **Camera placement** (part of staging) is the placement of the camera in order to achieve effective and compelling staging. In essence, camera placement is controlling the audience's eyes, deciding what an audience sees and does not see.

A visual storyteller must arrange all of her three-dimensional forms in such a way that they convey the story's meaning and reveal important information about the characters. A critical part of that arrangement is the placement of the camera. The following sections explain camera angles, lines of engagement, and the 180-degree rule. By understanding the meanings connoted by these devices, a visual storyteller can use camera placement as a powerful storytelling tool.

figure | 8-11 |

An extreme close-up of Mongo.

Camera Angle

Camera angle is the position of the camera in relation to the 3-D forms used while staging. Not all shots require the camera to be level with the subject or form. Just as altering the distance of the camera from the subject alters its meaning, altering the angle of the camera to the form changes how the audience perceives the images, objects, and actions on screen. Usually, camera angle refers to the camera placement being higher or lower than the character's eye level.

Straight-On Shot

A **straight-on shot** places the camera level with the object it is shooting. Here, the camera is approximately at eye level to an average human being. This shot allows the audience to feel like "an extra person in the room." The camera acts as the audience's perspective in the scene, and by placing the camera at eye level, the audience is invited to pretend that it is in the scene with the action and the characters. This is particularly useful in creating the empathic link between the audience and the character or events on screen.

| NOTE |

Remember that every choice about camera distance has an opportunity cost. The farther back the camera moves the grander the scope of the shot, but the greater the loss of detail. Conversely, the closer the camera is to the action the more detail is available for the audience, at the expense of visual context.

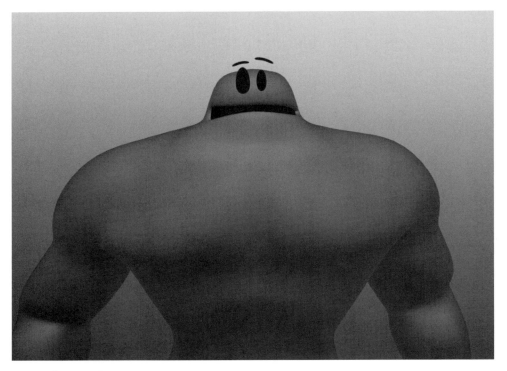

figure | 8–12 |

A straight-on shot of Mongo.

Up-Angle Shot

An **up-angle shot** places the camera below the level of the object, tilted up toward the object it is shooting. This produces the effect of forcing the audience into a subservient position. By dominating the audience with the shape, the shape gains scope, size, strength, and importance in the mind of the viewer. Up-angle shots are a useful tool when establishing that the perspective character defers to or fears the shape on screen. An up angle could be a dog's view of its owner or a person looking up at a formidable aggressor.

The up angle also allows the audience to feel sneaky if the shape on the screen does not acknowledge the camera. An audience's experience of the "sneaky" feeling can be one of delight at the ruse or, conversely, a deep experience of tension, suspense, or dread of discovery.

Down-Angle Shot

A **down-angle shot** places the camera above the level of the object, tilted down toward the object it is shooting. This produces the effect of forcing the audience into a dominant position. By elevating the audience above the shape, the shape becomes

figure | 8–13 |

An up-angle shot of Mongo.

manageable, innocent, and subservient to the viewer. This is a useful tool when establishing that the perspective character is meek, disempowered, or weak. A down angle could be the point of view of a parent or an avian. Once again, like the sneakiness of the up angle, if the character is oblivious to the camera, the audience feels as if it is spying on the action.

The down angle also allows the audience to feel powerful and deified, especially if the shape on screen acknowledges the camera. The audience's experience of being powerful over the subject can be a great tool for creating a genuinely compelling reversal later in the visual story or to reinforce a feeling of triumph over an adversary.

By varying the use of camera angles, the visual storyteller can maximize the emotional impact of a scene and keep longer sequences from growing stale. Like all tools, camera angles should be changed with intentionality and purpose. Camera angles should be motivated by the action on screen; the goal is to induce engagement, not nausea.

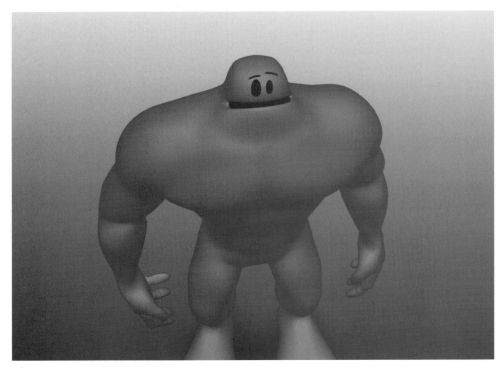

figure | 8–14 |

A down-angle shot of Mongo.

Line of Engagement

The **line of engagement** is the imaginary line along which the action takes place. If an imaginary line were drawn from the camera to the primary action, it would create a line of engagement. If two characters faced each other to speak, the line of engagement would be the imaginary line between their faces. Action must obey certain rules along this imaginary line in order to keep the meaning of events clear to the audience and to maximize their impact.

180-Degree Rule

The goal of staging is to arrange the three-dimensional elements of the scene in such a way that the events taking place are unmistakably clear in the final two-dimensional image. In order to achieve this goal it is important to understand the 180-degree rule.

The **180-degree rule** states that the camera should remain on one side of the line of engagement through a sequence. This means that the visual storyteller must choose a side of the line of engagement from which she will shoot the entire scene. So, when

figure | 8–15 |

Line of engagement.

Chip and Mongo race across the screen in pursuit of the goal, the camera is consistently on their right side. This results in the audience perceiving the two characters running from screen left to screen right in 2-D space. Any time there is a cut, the camera remains on the characters' right side, continuing the illusion that they are moving from screen left to screen right. What would happen if the 180-degree rule was broken and the camera was placed on the left side of the characters in the next frame? Suddenly, they would appear to be running in the opposite direction from screen right to screen left! So, even though the action remains the same in three-dimensional space, the camera placement has created a two-dimensional change in direction that confuses the audience.

To illustrate this point, if the camera is facing a pair of boxers in a ring, the camera should remain on the same side throughout the sequence. If the camera were to "hop" over their heads and come down on the other side of the boxers unannounced, then the audience would perceive that the boxers had switched sides (from their perspective) and wonder why it happened off screen.

Most screen time is dedicated to preserving and reinforcing the audience's sense of foundation and stability, which makes breaking the 180-degree rule detrimental to the goal of the scene. The result is often that the audience is "thrown out of the scene" and acutely aware that it is watching something pretend. The *dispelling of disbelief* breaks the fantasy and severely diminishes the impact of the story for the viewer. On the rare occasion that the visual storyteller wants the audience to be confused about action or to convey a sense of chaos or to disorient the viewer, breaking the 180-degree rule is an effective tool.

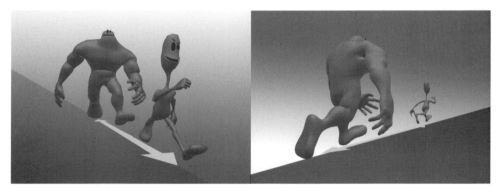

figure | 8-16 |

When a cut stays on the same side of the line of engagement, the audience can follow the action.

figure | 8-17 |

When the camera breaks the 180-degree rule by switching sides on the line of engagement, the audience becomes disoriented.

SUMMARY

Staging is the arranging of three-dimensional forms to create an effective two-dimensional composition, in other words, the presentation of any element in such a way that the element is completely clear. All of staging is encompassed in the arrangement of lines and shapes. The distance of the camera from the form influences the audience's perception of the form. Camera distance can be easily expressed as a long shot, full shot, medium shot, close-up, and extreme close-up. Camera placement (part of staging) is the placement of the camera in order to achieve staging. Camera angle is the position of the camera in relation to the 3-D forms used while staging. Camera angles can easily be expressed as straight-on, up-angle, or down-angle shots.

The line of engagement is the imaginary line along which the action takes place. If an imaginary line were drawn from the camera to the primary action, it would create a line of engagement. The 180-degree rule states that the camera should remain on one side of the line of engagement through a sequence.

in review

1. When is staging important?

2. What makes good staging?

3. Why is camera placement important?

4. What is the purpose of a long shot?

5. Which shots reveal the most information about a character's expression?

6. What camera angle views the subject from below?

7. Why should a visual storyteller be careful about breaking the 180-degree rule?

▶ *exercises*

1. Draw or film a character performing a specific action with a specific expression. Then redraw or reshoot that same image as a long shot, full shot, medium shot, close-up, and extreme close-up. Show the drawings or film to someone else and ask her to interpret the action in the image—ask what it means.

2. Draw or film a character performing a specific action with a specific expression. Then redraw or reshoot that same image from a variety of camera angles: straight on, up, and down angles. Show the drawings or film to someone else and ask her to interpret the action in the image—ask what it means.

3. Film two people approaching and moving past the camera. Film once following the 180-degree rule, and then film it again breaking the 180-degree rule. Can you think of a way to break the 180-degree rule in order to achieve a goal as a visual storyteller?

4. Stage a shot from straight-on, down-shot, and up-shot perspectives. Discuss how the different angles on the same subjects change the "feel" of the shots.

CHAPTER 9

"All the world's a stage. . . ."
—William Shakespeare (1564–1616)
As You Like It, Act II, scene vii

"In order to have a complete description of the motion, we must specify how the body alters its position with time."
—Albert Einstein (1879–1955)
Relativity: The Special and General Theory Albert Einstein (1879–1955). Relativity: The Special and General Theory. 1920. III. *Space and Time in Classical Mechanics 3rd paragraph* - http://www.bartleby.com/173/3.html

objectives

- Examine methods for thinking in terms of editing
- Define the difference between linear and nonlinear editing
- Enumerate the questions that audiences bring to the screen
- Explore the concept of pure cinema

key terms

editing	linear editing	audience questions
subjective camera	nonlinear editing	pure cinema

INTRODUCTION TO STAGING OVER TIME

A majority of *Exploring Visual Storytelling* has been dedicated to explaining how specific moments and shot composition are used to create compelling stories. These tools are critical, however, none of them happen in a vacuum; they occur in the context of the events that precede and follow. The journey from one bit of context to the next (which is necessary to give meaning to events) happens over time. Given that visual storytelling exists in a time-based media, the use of and control of this time is one of the more potent visual storytelling tools. In much the same way that an image can be given a wide variety of meaning by simply altering camera placement in relation to the image, so too does the process of ordering shots alter their meaning to the audience. The awareness of shot order is the first step in the larger skill of editing.

EDITING HAPPENS BEFORE YOU SHOOT

Editing is the decision of "which pieces of context" to supply for the audience. Therefore, editing must take place before the visual storyteller captures the first frame of action. Editing is not simply a post-production process where completed clips of footage are chopped up, rearranged, and combined with sound effects and added transitions. Editing is also a pre-production process in which the visual storyteller decides where to place the camera, what will appear on the screen, and what length of time any given element will remain focal.

A visual storyteller must always be mindful of *what* he plans to show and what he plans to hide from the audience. This selection process is important because each piece of new context alters the meaning of onscreen events. The concept that whenever the camera shows one thing, it omits a deal more is known as **subjective camera.** Like human eyes, the greater the focus, the larger the area of ignorance. If a person places his eye up to a microscope, he is given tremendous amounts of information about the object under the lens. He is also effectively blinded to everything else in the room. By focusing on one thing, others are ignored. The attempt to view everything involves the loss of detail. This choice of value is the choice of subjective camera. A visual storyteller must remember that whenever he draws focus, he also creates blindness.

By choosing to place the camera on a flat and level plane with Chip and Mongo as they finally relax on the catwalk, the visual storyteller has chosen to allow the audience to relax and feel safe. The visual storyteller has subjectively decided not to show the flames building below in the pit or the rotating knives poised to jut forth. The choice is rooted in the desire to surprise the characters (and simultaneously the audience) with the sudden arrival of danger (flames and knives). Since the audience had no reason to suspect the arrival of the danger, the impact of the reversal from calm to panic, from safety to dangerous, is stronger. The best visual storytellers manipulate the subjective camera in order to maximize the impact of the story beats.

| NOTE |

The best visual storytellers manipulate the subjective camera in order to maximize the impact of the story beats.

figure | 9–1 |

The choice to place the camera inside the rotating knives maximizes the threat of danger.

Editing Pre-Visualizes the Final Product

An editor cannot edit footage that does not exist. The footage will not exist until someone shoots it. The best way to capture proper footage in the first place is to anticipate the post-production process and visualize the visual story in its finished form. Thus, details of what will appear on screen are best worked out before principal photography begins. More than a focus on pre-production, this is the pre-visualization of post-production and the final cut. When the end-goal of the visual story is clearly articulated by the visual storyteller, then everyone involved can work efficiently toward the goal with all efforts focused in the same direction. Without this deeper understanding of the final product (or editing process), the efforts of production will be haphazard, frustrated, and redundant. The production is very likely to run over time and over budget, and the outcomes are unpredictable.

When deciding which shots to include and which to exclude, each shot should be subjected to the following questions:

- Exposition: does each shot achieve a goal and advance the audience's understanding of the information and feeling?

- Context: does the shot inform the audience about how to feel about the previous and following shot?

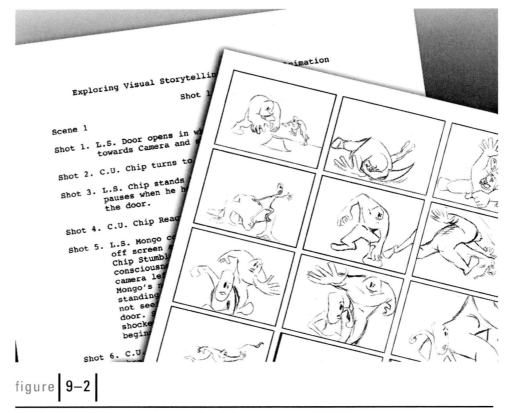

figure | 9–2 |

Pre-visualization is part of anticipating the editing process.

- Continuity: does this shot align with the main ideas sewn into the fabric of the story (or is it just neat)?

The answers to these questions allow the visual storyteller to edit (make decisions regarding) each element that appears on screen as well as determine their most effective chronological order.

If a shot fails to advance the character or story by delivering new information, then it should be revised or omitted. If it fails to supply the audience with clues about how to feel about events on screen, it should be revised or omitted. If a shot provides information that is accidentally contradictory or inconsistent with information delivered earlier, then it needs to be revised or omitted. If a shot provides very little new or important information, then the information should be combined into another, more robust shot.

Linear and Nonlinear Editing

Linear editing is the process of arranging the shots in the same order that they occurred in the chronology of the story. First things are shown before second things, and so on. The audience first sees a chicken laying an egg. The egg hatches and reveals a chick. The chick plays with other chicks. The chick grows up and becomes Emperor Fluffyrumples, lord of the coop.

Linear editing allows the audience to feel like it is experiencing events in the same way that its empathic character experiences them. It feels "natural."

Nonlinear editing is the process of showing the audience shots out of the order they occurred in the chronology of the story. It basically encompasses any order other than time-based sequence. The audience first sees Fluffyrumples, the supreme emperor of the coop. The next shot reveals the laying of the egg that will become Fluffyrumples; this still makes sense to the audience but the events are shown to the audience out of order. By showing events differently from the order in which they took place in the real time of the story, the visual storyteller is trading the audience's satisfaction at the hero achieving a particular goal for the anticipation and possible tension that will color the events during the story.

Skipping around in time allows the visual storyteller to reveal new context to the audience in an order that is most important to the viewers' emotional experience of events rather than the literal chronological order of events.

Now, let us take the concept of editing context over time and explore the labyrinth sequence in the animation. For example, the labyrinth sequence can be broken down into a few key sections. The first section is when Chip and Mongo make a decision about the labyrinth; in this scenario each is deciding how he is going to face the obstacle.

Chip has decided to run his way through the maze and "figure" his way to the other side, while Mongo has decided to "blast" his way through.

Characters solve problems according to their strengths.

Their actions culminate with Chip almost reaching his goal just as Mongo barrels in, causing the goal to once again slip beyond the reach of them both.

The important thing to understand as a visual storyteller is that there is no "labyrinth."

figure | 9–3 |

Chip and Mongo enter the labyrinth, beginning the labyrinth sequence in chronological order.

figure | 9–4 |

Chip escapes the labyrinth using wit.

figure | 9–5 |

Mongo escapes the labyrinth using force.

figure | 9–6 |

There is no labyrinth; there is a series of shots that creates the illusion of the labyrinth.

Chip does not literally take all the steps necessary to navigate his way through the entire labyrinth, and Mongo does not literally punch down every single wall in his way. The shots in this sequence are simply arranged in a way that gives the impression of those events taking place yet avoids all of the time-consuming detail of real-life events.

The labyrinth scene begins with a decision sequence. The camera is placed on the side of engagement that shows the characters' faces as they contemplate the best way to navigate the labyrinth ahead. Having chosen the line of engagement, the camera is placed in front of Chip and Mongo, and the only thing that changes between the direct shots of each of them is the direction of the camera. The camera's location remains constant, in front of the two characters.

Once Chip decides to leave Mongo and try his luck in the labyrinth, the camera moves further down the corridor to track his movement but remains on the same side of the line of engagement as it was in the beginning of the scene. When Chip rounds the corner, the scenario has changed. This allows the line of engagement to change without confusing the viewer. In this particular sequence, the character (Chip) changes directions, but the camera remains constantly on the same side of the line of engagement. The goal of the shot is to show Chip maneuvering through the maze, so by showing Chip move from screen left to screen right, then from screen right to screen left, the audience can appreciate the complexity of his decisions about how to solve the labyrinth's maze. Camera angles are used to full effect in the creation of these shots. The same location can be shot from a new angle, allowing the visual storyteller to have an additional asset without creating or scouting a new location.

Mongo's situation is the exact opposite of Chip's. Mongo chooses one direction and heads that way through the entire labyrinth. As a result of this choice, Mongo is always going from screen left to screen right. This situation changes in the final sequence of the labyrinth when Mongo bursts through the wall from screen right.

By reversing Mongo's direction in 2-D space, his arrival becomes more surprising for not only Chip but the audience as well.

figure | **9–7** |

A camera move can help heighten the feeling of surprise.

THE AUDIENCE'S THREE QUESTIONS

Editing, or the arrangement of shots, is done to answer three **audience questions**, which an audience asks of every visual story: what is going on, who is involved, and how to feel about it.

Every scene needs a goal, which is best thought of as the reason the visual storyteller created the scene in the first place. The goal of a scene sounds something like "This is the scene where the protagonist reveals his love for the heroine or the audience learns that the mysterious stranger is actually the duke's son or teenager Timmy finally gets his hotrod to run or the audience finally gets to know the quirky family and establish its affection for birds."

The purpose or goal of each of these scenes is the reason they exist, and each shot is a step toward showing these intangible ideas to the audience with enough context to give them meaning. In order for the audience to comprehend the goal of the scene, the three previous questions must be clearly answered. The audience member only sees the world through the visual storyteller's eyes. In order for him to enter the world and experience the story as the character, he has to feel comfortable and safe. That feeling of safety and comfort is only achieved when the audience knows:

- Where it is in the physical world of the story

- What the action on screen appears to be

- How it should feel about the events unfolding on screen

With these three foundations in place, the audience is ready and eager to believe the story as it unfolds. Paradoxically, audience members, like all people, are only comfortable with risk and change when they feel safe. Answering the three audience questions allows the audience to feel safe enough to risk participating in the delightful lie of the story.

What Is Going On?

"What's going on," or exposition, is a fundamental goal (and the most basic level) of storytelling. No good visual story fails to answer this question in order to root the audience firmly in the facts of events. But good visual stories also supply the audience with additional layers of meaning and context. Audiences are filled with people who contradictorily crave the feeling of safety while taking the imagined risk of believing a lie. The audience's feeling of safety comes from knowing what is going on at any moment in the visual story. With this safety in place, the audience feels comfortable imagining what will be going on soon and reflects on the meaning of what went on in the past few scenes. This process of anticipation and reflection are only options when

figure | 9–8 |

The audience needs to know *where the scene takes place.*

pondering from the safety of knowing where it is *now*. The knowledge of *what is going on* enables the audience to see the visual story as a whole, rather than a series of isolated incidents.

The primary tool a visual storyteller uses to solidify *what is going on* in the mind of the audience is context. By showing the audience an establishing shot, *place* is established. An establishing shot of the desert tells the audience that the scene will occur in the desert, therefore rocks, sand, and cacti are evidence of place, not necessarily critical elements to the story (though in a good visual story the location is an externalization of a character's internal state). By showing the audience a full shot of a person, *character* is established. When action begins and shots get tighter, the audience can use information gathered from the wider shots to extrapolate *what is going on* in the tighter shots. A tight shot of an established desert-dwelling character greedily gulping water has more meaning than the same shot without the context established by the wider shots.

By establishing characteristics for any element on screen, the audience can be armed with the tools it needs to give meaning to the actions when it lacks the full context of a wide shot. The shot of the burning paper airplane pushing the red button to end the danger to Mongo would be meaningless without context. The audience would not know *what is going on* unless what was going on had been properly established earlier. With context and the knowledge of where it is, the audience can understand what is going on; in this case, Chip has achieved his goal of saving Mongo by using a skill he demonstrated earlier in the visual story.

Who Is Involved?

"Who's involved?" is a slightly higher level of "what's going on." The audience still needs to feel safe about viewing the fantastic lie of a visual story, so it needs to know who is on screen and be able to tell them apart from other characters. If audience members are to establish a link with any of the characters on screen, they must be able to trust that they know who they are viewing. In the same way that naming characters similarly is confusing for the audience because of the lack of contrast—Jim, Jimmy, James, and Jake would be hard character names to track—half a dozen characters of similar size, shape, coloring, and mannerisms would make great soldiers marching in lockstep, but horribly difficult characters to differentiate on screen.

Chip and Mongo are exercises in emphasized contrast with the goal of making it clear to the audience who is who. For example, Chip is short and skinny, Mongo is tall and thick. Chip is small and quick, Mongo is large and slow. Chip is selfish and skittish, Mongo is generous and calm. These contrasts translate into behavioral opposites on screen, which make it easier for the audience to differentiate who it is watching. So, when a quick and thin blue arm reaches for the goal, we know it is Chip's, while a slow ham-fisted blue grip on the goal belongs to Mongo.

When the audience feels confident that it knows who it is watching, it is able to apply a series of expectations and context to the action on screen. When the audience fails to comprehend who is on screen, it is thrust out of the story and left wondering what it is watching. Audience members will eventually ask themselves whether they should continue watching at all. The experience of being thrown out of the story is one of the few things an audience member will not forgive the visual storyteller. Audience members who are confident in the identities of the key players are lulled into a joyous suspension of disbelief. Audience members who are unsure of the key players quickly devolve into an angry mob.

How Should I Feel about It?

An audience takes its cues for how to feel about a shot from the unique execution of events presented by the visual storyteller. Character actions, character dialogue, shot composition, and lighting and pacing all inform the audience how to feel about the action on screen. A visual storyteller's job is not to *tell* an audience what to *think* about what it sees on screen, but to *show* the audience how to *feel* about it. This is achieved through a variety of visual and audio clues.

| NOTE |

A visual storyteller's job is not to tell an audience *what to think* about what it sees on screen, but to show the audience *how to feel* about it.

figure | 9–9 |

Audiences will not listen until they have felt a connection to the story.

Dialogue is the easiest way to let the audience know how to feel about what it views on screen. If a character with whom the audience empathizes expresses a particular feeling about an event, then the audience knows that it is expected to feel the same. If a character with whom the audience lacks sympathy expresses a feeling about an event, the audience is skeptical. Good dialogue does not state the way that the character (and therefore the audience) feels about an event, but implies it indirectly. A character who loses his true love may speak bitterly, "Now I can finally go to the fish restaurant that my true love hated," and the audience can still understand from the context of the enormity of the loss that the character is not actually happy. The character is suffering and sad, therefore the audience should feel sad, too. The audience knows not to take the words literally and rejoice in the new dining options, but grieves along with the character and his loss. By implying the proper emotion for the audience, the dialogue grows richer and the audience has a clear direction.

Composition also informs the audience how to feel about a shot. By carefully manipulating the camera angle, lighting, and the arrangement of elements on screen, the visual storyteller can change the feeling about events on screen. Properly composed and contextualized, a small child offering a lollipop can be the picture of innocence or, with the audience's knowledge that the sucker is poisonous, a terrifying and foreboding moment.

WHAT DOES THIS SHOT DO?

Good shots are like good newspapers. Each new shot needs to deliver new information to the audience or it grows bored and flips to the comics. When a visual storyteller begins to think of new shots in terms of delivering new information, the question of shot order disappears and is replaced by the question, what does the audience need to know next?

A visual storyteller creates a new shot to reveal at least one new piece of information to the audience. The new information should be important to either the character's understanding of his world or the audience's. The information does not have to be profound. "The fire is hot . . ." is just as good as "The murderer is. . . ."

Each shot should show the audience a new nuance of character, location, or event that was not available to it before. An establishing shot lets the audience know where it is. A full shot lets the audience know who the characters are. A close shot might reveal a small action, reveal the time, or let the audience see something that another character does not. Regardless, each new shot exists to reveal new information to the audience in a way that allows it to feel secure in the fictional journey.

PURE CINEMA

Pure cinema refers to the idea that action and reaction must combine in order to create meaning. Actions have no meaning in a vacuum, and character reactions are meaningless devoid of context. It is the presence of extra personal events and characters that grant meaning to actions and reactions, not the action or the reaction alone.

Ultimately, context is the choice of visual selection. Therefore, context is the key to pure cinema. The visual storyteller chooses which images appear on screen, in which order they appear, and their distance from the camera. Every one of those subjective editing decisions contributes to the cinematic experience of the audience.

Everything that is *shown* on screen is more powerful than what is *told*. Showing character actions and reactions (the essence of pure cinema) is more compelling than telling the audience about them. Every choice the visual storyteller makes about what to show and what to tell gives his story unique context that stylizes his stories and differentiates them from others.

Mongo raising his eyebrows in a medium shot is meaningless. Mongo raising his eyebrows in reaction to seeing Chip swoop in and swipe the goal out from under him has meaning. The audience knows how it should feel about Chip grabbing the goal because of Mongo's reaction to the external action.

| NOTE |

Each new shot exists to reveal new information to the audience in a way that allows it to feel secure in the fictional journey.

figure | 9-10 |

Reactions are meaningless without knowing the actions that cause them.

SUMMARY

Editing is the decision of "which pieces of context" to supply for the audience. Therefore, if a coherent story is to be made, editing must take place before the visual storyteller captures the first frame of action. A visual storyteller must always keep in mind that his choice to show or not to show utterly alters the meaning of the events shown. This is known as subjective camera.

Shots are arranged to communicate to the audience "What's going on," "Who's involved," and "How to feel about it." A visual storyteller's job is not to tell an audience what to think about what it sees on screen, but rather to show the audience how to feel about it.

Shots are a lot like newspapers. Each shot needs to deliver new information to the audience or it grows bored and flips to the comics. When a visual storyteller begins to understand that delivering new information is the reason for a new shot, this problem solves itself. Pure cinema refers to the idea that action and reaction must combine in order to create meaning.

in review

1. What is the purpose of making the audience feel safe?

2. Why should the visual storyteller begin editing before shooting the first frame?

3. What kinds of stories lend themselves to linear versus nonlinear formats?

4. Why does the audience need to know who is on screen?

5. What happens to the audience when any of the "three questions" go unanswered?

exercises

1. Retell a popular fairy tale, but rearrange the sequence of events and tell it out of chronological order.

2. Stage a showdown between two gunslingers and shoot it with the camera in the best place to capture all the information. Experiment with camera distance. Are there some distances that keep the audience from answering the three questions?

3. Create a complex storyline and then draw random images from the story and show them around. Ask people what they see. Now, explain the whole story and show them the images again. Ask them what they see in the images now.

4. Pick a popular visual story and ask of it three questions, "What's going on?" "Who's involved?" and "How should I feel about it?" Looking at these answers, can you think of any other visual stories that have similar answers? Can you think of your own visual story that raises the stakes of the story you studied and makes it more interesting?

CHAPTER 10

"It is evident that there is a principle of connection between the different thoughts or ideas of the mind . . . this is so observable that . . . even in our . . . wandering reveries, nay in our very dreams, we shall find, if we reflect, that the imagination ran not altogether at adventures, but that there was still a connection upheld among the different ideas, which succeeded each other."

—David Hume (1711–1776)

objectives

- Examine story-shaping tools
- Explore brainstorming tools

figure | 10–1 |

How do you know if you have a great idea for a visual story?

INTRODUCTION TO STORY-SHAPING

Story-shaping is the kind of big-picture thinking required to lay a solid foundation for a visual story. Neat characters, cool traits, awesome locations, plot twists, and surprise endings are all building materials. While a wooden frame has a certain kind of majesty, a pile of lumber lying on the ground has no dignity whatsoever. This chapter is dedicated to providing tools that are useful in building a framework to hold your creativity in a way that makes it accessible and exciting for the audience to experience.

HOW DO WE PUT ALL THIS TOGETHER?

A puzzle can be assembled in nearly any order so long as the end result forms the intended picture. While this is true, there are ways to assemble a puzzle that make it come together faster. For example, lining up all the edge pieces first gives the puzzler a framework for the puzzle and provides context for the rest of the pieces. The same is true for visual storytelling.

figure | 10–2 |

A visual storyteller needs to be able to ask the right questions to get the right answers.

The edge pieces in a visual story are a compelling character. Once armed with a compelling character, the visual storyteller then has the puzzle piece that will inform the placement of all the other pieces. The obstacles will be constructed in such a way that they sincerely challenge the main character to change. The placement of these obstacles will become the plot. The obstacle characters and supporting characters will populate the world of the story, and their combined motives and goals will shape the context in which the story takes place. The visual storyteller will decide on a perspective character from the new population of her world.

If the edge pieces give just enough information to spot color trends in the puzzle image, then the character gives just enough information to create the obstacles, and the obstacles in turn give just enough information to inform the other characters, the other characters give just enough information to inform the plot—and so on.

A consistent mood and tone will evolve from the rapidly forming picture and a through line will emerge that can be used to ferret out ideas that do not fit the master picture. What begins as a pile of irregular shapes can coalesce into one clear and coherent shape; a visual story.

MORE ABOUT BRAINSTORMING

Everyone is capable of coming up with solid ideas around which a story can be fashioned. Here are some quick tips that can help to jumpstart the brainstorming process. Assuming you are going to start with *character*, you need to observe a few interesting ones to stimulate your imagination. The easiest and most accessible characters are friends, coworkers, and family members. Re-envision all your years of social interactions into a fictitious character that is an amalgam of everything odd, funny, outrageous, and uncomfortable about your extended family, friends, and coworkers.

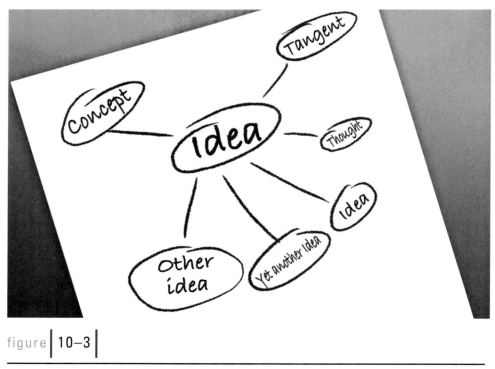

figure | 10-3 |

A brainstorm cluster.

If your immediate circle of personal contacts fails to yield colorful character inspirations, try going to the places interesting people gather to talk. Here you may observe (notice that stalking was never advocated here) conversations and personalities that are outside your normal sphere. Exposure to a fresh set of mannerisms, values, habits, and personalities can be a solid source of inspiration. A quick list of places that fit the bill includes:

- Late night eateries or any place open twenty-four hours a day

- Special interest groups

- City events open to the public—state fair, Department of Motor Vehicles, and so on

Go to places that offer fresh perspectives and jot down anything that sticks in your memory—odd conversations, mannerisms, modes of speech, clothes, conversation topics, or distinctive behaviors. Anything that captures your attention will likely intrigue an audience. Imagine a character that has these interesting traits and write out a little biography for her. This biography can be a few paragraphs or a bulleted list of traits, but remember, external traits such as height, weight, and shoe size are not a character; they are characteristics. Internal traits such as values and motives are character.

The biggest thing to remember when you are brainstorming is that it is not a concrete or linear process. It is also not any place for an editor; do not let anyone, including yourself, censor the brainstorming process. All ideas are presumed innocent until proven useless.

The processes of brainstorming take a wide variety of forms that can include:

- Staring out the window and thinking about your idea

- Pitching your rough ideas to your friends or mentors

- Watching visual stories with similar elements to your idea

- Making doodles of your character

- Flipping through a phone book for good character names

- Throwing out your first seven hundred ideas

For more information on "how to create pre-production," find a book or series of books dedicated to the particular subsection of pre-production such as screenwriting or storyboarding.

STORY-BUILDING PROMPTS

Often a visual storyteller has a keen instinct that tells her that something is missing, but that instinct is not always forthcoming about the exact nature of the malady. Here are a hundred questions to ask yourself whenever a story feels void of something. Think of each question as a swift kick in the brain that can shake loose the dust of indecision in order to reveal the compelling story underneath.

1. Who is the main character? What does she value?

2. Why should the audience be interested in her?

3. What makes or allows the audience to empathize with her?

4. Why can't she get what she craves for?

5. What are the character's hopes, desires, and dreams?

6. What does the main character want and need (on an emotional and subconscious level)?

7. How can the temptations be made more irresistible and the stakes higher?

8. How can the internal and external obstacles become more insurmountable?

9. How can the threat or dangers become more excruciating, agonizing, or humiliating?

10. Does the time period reflect the environment? How? What expresses the period besides costumes, props, architecture, and means of transportation and communication? How does it reflect our human attitudes, habits, customs, social events, rituals, and language?

11. What is the moment that the audience becomes ultimately curious about? What does it impatiently expect? What does it realize will happen when the moment comes?

12. Why exactly should the audience find a character sympathetic?

13. What makes the audience curious about her? What is her mystery? Magic? Charisma? What does it look like to the audience?

14. What do audience members find in her story that is relevant to them?

15. Why exactly should the audience identify with her?

16. What is the passionate secret desire of the main character?

17. What does the audience hope for?

18. What is the audience afraid of?

19. What is the worst thing that could and will happen to her?

20. What is the most auspicious, bright moment that she will experience in the story?

21. What is she going to lose if she does not find a way to surmount her adversities?

22. Why will the character lose self-respect or piece of mind if she does not get what she wants?

23. What can be done to eliminate the audience's disbelief in the first act?

24. Is there a deadline (time lock) for the action to come to a resolution? Could there be? Who can create it?

25. When and how does the main character realize that she is in trouble and must extricate herself?

26. What are the imaginable alternative storylines?

27. How can the problem be solved? How can it appear impossible?

28. Who or what makes the goal unattainable?

29. Can the forced action be evaded? What would happen if it were? What makes the evasion possible?

30. Can the complication be ignored, ridiculed, forgotten? Make sure it cannot be. Can it be solved on friendly terms? Who will sabotage it?

31. Who can the main character rely on? Who does she hope to get on her side?

32. What doesn't she anticipate or know about?

33. What does she (falsely) expect will happen?

34. Will the audience understand why the characters act as they do?

35. How do the characters rationalize their moves?

36. How does the audience get to know a character's particular intentions, motives, desires, and hopes?

37. How can the next step that the character takes lead to unexpected results?

38. What is the miscalculation?

39. What did the antagonistic character do to thwart the goal?

40. Who threaten or try to humiliate, stop, ridicule, or destroy her plans?

41. How did the circumstances change after plans were made?

42. How can the goal be made more desirable? Who can do that?

43. What can create the situations, doubts, or scruples in the character's mind?

44. Try to imagine all the locations that the character can enter in pursuit of her objective or to evade the dangers. Are there some more interesting sites? Places more contradictory to the situation?

45. What are the emotions, conclusions, and decisions that result from the setback, failure, and complication?

46. What emotions does an insult, mistreatment, or injustice evoke? Show the effect of these events on character emotionally. Are they best shown privately or publicly?

47. What danger, what abyss, becomes visible for the audience that the hero does not see?

48. What are audience expectations after the first obstacle is overcome? What does the audience hope for or wish the character would do? Why can't they do it?

49. What is the hero's biggest error, intentional blunder?

50. How does the protagonist react to the antagonist's moves? Does the hero panic? Feel alarmed? Diffident? Horrified from the realization of what could happen?

51. What happens that helps the protagonist? What about the antagonist?

52. Which character has the audience underestimated?

53. What characters can act as catalyst to alter or increase reactions of the antagonist or protagonist?

54. Which character(s) can go through a similar plight and find a different solution, compromise, assimilation, rejection, and so on?

55. What relationships become threatened? Broken up? Transformed?

56. What consequences of the previous actions can aggravate the situation?

57. What are the places the main character does not want to go? Afraid to go? How is she forced to go?

58. What is the prevailing mood of the whole story?

59. Does the environment have a face, character, and temperament?

60. Are the events sufficiently important and impressionable? Do they help to eliminate the lifestyle, engagement, and involvement of the character?

61. Does the main character show naïveté? Weaknesses? Disbelief?

62. Does she reevaluate everything she has done?

63. Does she regret? Recriminate? Seek consolation?

64. Does she reject the original plan?

65. Are all possibilities of self-assurance, shrewdness, foresightedness, and wisdom that the hero can possess exhausted?

66. What precautions does the hero take? Does she look for advice? Help?

67. What new plans does she come up with? How does she acquire new courage?

68. What or who can suggest a new stratagem for her?

69. How does she study the adversary?

70. Does she discover the weaknesses of the antagonist? Or is she wrong in her assumption?

71. What trap can both sides set? How can they attack each other? How can she test the enemy?

72. How does inner turmoil grow in the minds of the characters? How does it embitter their antagonism?

73. How does the visual storyteller feel about the rhythm of the story?

74. Does the tempo of the main action accelerate?

75. What can interrupt, temporarily stop, misdirect, or confuse the growing conflict?

76. Are the chances for the desired resolution and for the abhorred outcome equal?

77. Is the resolution becoming inevitable? What could reverse this course of action?

78. What hopes still remain for the main character after a setback?

79. What are the most feared confrontations that she tries in vain to avoid, postpone, deny?

80. What is the most humiliating, painful extremity the hero will experience?

81. What is the moment when the antagonist feels triumphant?

82. How can you increase the adversary's determination not to give up, not to show any restraint, to fight to the bitter end?

83. How can good or bad timing heighten the stakes (too early or too late, speeding up the plans)?

84. When does the hero realize the inevitability of the outcome?

85. Can an appeal be made to the antagonist's better nature? Can the fear of shame, disgrace of losing face be used?

86. How did the circumstances change to make the outcome weightier, impressive, and convincing?

87. Does anybody admit errors? Does anybody plead, beg forgiveness, and confess?

88. Is anybody willing to give up? Is anybody trying to escape?

89. Does anybody feel shame, disgrace, insecurity, betraying one's most cherished principals? Does anybody feel terror stricken of being exposed?

90. Are any of the adversaries rescued? Is it possible? For what price?

91. Is there a moment when a conscience-stricken character realizes the consequences of her actions, sees her situation accurately, and tries to stop the inevitable?

92. Has the concept been mined for all its ins and outs? Nuances? Messages?

93. What possible events could happen believably and properly in your chosen environment? What possible events would be unusual, out of the routine order?

94. Do the antagonists know about the secret desires of the main character? What are their plans? What tactics do they use? What mimicry, subterfuge? How do they try to mislead, misdirect, confuse the main character? What are their hopes, desires, and dreams? What do they want, need? How do they rationalize their moves? How can their obstinacy, rage, hatred, hurt self-esteem, and ambition be fueled? What can help them to feel righteous or at least fairly treated?

95. Does the antagonist mobilize herself or her forces? Does she set a trap? Does she try to confuse the main character? What are the social reasons for her actions? Does she come with accusations? Direct lies? Does she outwit the main character?

96. Does the antagonist get a chance to show her intelligence, vigilance, alertness?

97. Does act I foreshadow events in act II and act III?

98. Is the character arc as dynamic as possible?

99. What if the perspective character changed? How would it change the story?

100. Do you, the visual storyteller, feel love for every single character?

VISUAL PROMPTS

Here are ten foundational questions to ask yourself when you feel that your visuals are not having the intended impact on the audience.

1. Exposition: does each shot achieve a goal and advance the audience's understanding of the information and feeling?

2. Context: does the shot inform the audience about how to feel about the previous and following shot?

3. Continuity: does this shot align with the main ideas sewn into the fabric of the story, or is it just neat?

4. What is going on in a shot?

5. Who is involved in a shot?

6. How should the audience feel about the shot?

7. What is the goal of the scene?

8. Is location firmly established?

9. Is the audience's eye drawn to the primary action?

10. Is it clear what is "happening" in the shot? In the scene?

As with any artistic pursuit, the possibilities of visual storytelling are virtually limitless. However, if you spend time practicing and applying the techniques, tools, and principles contained in *Exploring Visual Storytelling*, you are well on your way to creating work that is both clear and compelling.

glossary

180-degree rule: A rule that states that the camera should remain on one side of the line of engagement throughout a sequence.

2-D camera space: The canvas on which the visual storyteller paints three-dimensional ideas onto a two-dimensional surface; it has height and width.

3-D space: The normal space of the world. Everything has three dimensions height, width, and depth; also called three-dimensional space.

act: A story structure model composed of key plot points and used to indicate beginning, middle, and end.

action: In screenplay terms, it refers to anything the audience will see or hear (not including dialogue); in storyboarding terms, it is an individual component of an activity.

antagonist: The character who most actively opposes the (protagonist) hero's goals; otherwise known as the villain.

audience: The intended receiver of a visual story.

beat: A singular moment in the story usually taking the form of an action or reaction; also see *story beat*.

brainstorming: The random processing of ideas from the brain, in no specific order and with no apparent logic.

brevity: Conciseness of expression; it is always the visual storyteller's goal.

camera angle: The position of the camera in relation to the 3-D forms used while staging.

camera distance: The distance of the camera to a shape.

camera placement: The placement of the camera in order to achieve staging.

catalyst: The forces that motivate change or action in a character.

catharsis: The purification or purgation that releases tension from a person or elicits a spiritual renewal; occurs in audience when a character overcomes an obstacle.

character: An entity that represents a particular perspective or set of experiences, usually someone who receives a name in the story.

character arc: The process of a character facing challenges and experiencing personal change in order to overcome external obstacles.

character lock: The series of obstacles and events that conspire to eliminate character choice; the result of this lock-in is ultimately forced action.

climax: The moment when the stakes of a visual story are as high as they can possibly get; a ten on a scale of one to ten.

close-up: A shot that shows how a character feels about a situation; it usually only includes the emotive part of the body.

color and light: Used to create contrast.

composition: The arrangement of lines and shapes in camera space.

concept-forming: Part of the brain-storming process, where the visual story-teller begins to sort ideas by various similarities.

conflict: What occurs when two forces with mutually exclusive goals meet.

context: Establishes the relationship between characters and events or objects and people, in order to give actions emotional meaning for the audience.

contrast: In the visual arts, elements that differ in order to bring clarity to each other; contrast makes elements dynamic and interesting.

cut: The transition formed when one frame is followed by another that does not take place in the (relatively) same time or place.

decision: An externalized moment of clarity and growth when a character decides to either accept or reject pressure for change.

depth: The ability for an image element to have distance from the camera.

dialogue: Words spoken by characters.

dominant shape: The shape that is larger or higher on the screen than another; the audience infers that the shape is threatening.

down angle: When the camera is above the level of the objects and tilted down toward the object it is shooting.

dynamic range: The degree to which details of a character, scene, or emotion change from the beginning to the end.

dynamic tension: The degree to which the audience is provoked to feel relaxation or intensity between the beginning and the end of a scene or story.

edit: See *editing.*

editing: The decision of "which pieces of context" to supply for the audience.

emotional experience: To evoke a feeling from the audience, which is a visual storyteller's goal.

empathic link: A feeling of empathy between the audience and the character(s).

establishing shot: A shot that sets the location of the scene.

event: Something that happens in a story, a plot point.

exposition: The stating of facts.

externalize: To make visible something that is inherently invisible (intangible).

extreme close-up: A shot that shows detailed action or emotion; usually includes a subject so small it could not be seen in longer shots.

fade out: When a shot fades down to 0 percent visibility while a black screen fades up to 100 percent visibility. A fade in is the reverse.

forced action: The kinds of action that take place because the character has no choice if he wishes to continue pursuing his goals.

forced change: The process by which a character either adapts himself to or alters his surroundings in order to overcome an obstacle.

form: A shape in three-dimensional space.

frame: A single, still image; film shot at twenty-four frames per second creates the illusion of movement.

full shot: A shot that reveals the character's entire body; it is designed to show the character's actions.

goal: Something a character wants and has yet to attain.

hero: The character who embodies the ideals of his world; sometimes known as the main character or protagonist.

implied line: A repetition of linear elements constructed in such a way as to imply a line; not a literal or unbroken line.

intangible: An idea, thought, or feeling that does not naturally appear as something a person can hear or see.

line: A two-dimensional construct that has length but virtually no depth or width. There are no lines in three-dimensional spaces, where lines become forms.

line of engagement: The imaginary line along which the action takes place.

line orientation: The direction or angle of the visual pathway.

linear editing: The process of arranging the shots in the same order that they occurred in the chronology of the story.

location: The physical setting in which an event takes place; an externalization designed to actively challenge the character.

long shot: A shot that shows the character in relationship to his surroundings and involves the camera being "far" from the subject.

main character: The character who either changes himself or his world the most from the beginning to the end of the story; also called a hero or protagonist. (See *character*.)

medium shot: A shot that shows the character's upper body or portion of the character's body and is designed to show more subtle action.

mentor: An older character (usually not a parent) that provides guidance and inspiration as a supporting character.

nonlinear: See *nonlinear editing*.

nonlinear editing: The process of showing the audience shots out of the order that they occurred in the chronology of the story.

obstacle: Roadblocks between the character and his goals, taking the form of people, beliefs, geography, or society.

obstacle character: Character(s) who work actively to oppose the protagonist's goals.

outline: A succinct summary of key events.

passion: The motivated and caring aspect of talent; it is the level of attraction a person has for a task.

payoff information: When an audience is able to use planted information to give events meaning.

perspective character: The character through whose experience the story unfolds—not always the main character or protagonist.

pitching: The act of standing in front of a live audience and sharing a passion for the visual story by speaking and directing the audience's attention through the beats of the storyboard.

planting information: The technique of invisibly providing the audience with important context.

plot: A series of events designed to actively challenge the character to change.

post-production: The process of altering source audio or video by editing or applying effects.

pre-production: The detailed planning of the work you will produce.

primary element: An action so significant that it requires its own storyboard panel.

production: The actual creation of the media content.

protagonist: The main character or hero, who works hardest toward a goal and either changes the most or changes the world the most while pursuing the goal.

pure cinema: Refers to the idea that action and reaction must combine in order to create meaning.

realization: An externalized moment of clarity and change when a character realizes something fundamental to his success against obstacles.

rule of three (acts): A three-act structure provides the most familiar framework for audiences to relate to a story.

rule of three (scenes): Scenes, like stories, should have a beginning, middle, and end.

rule of three (story): Highly recognized stories are told in a three-act structure with a beginning, middle, and end.

scene: All that happens on screen until there is a significant change of time or place.

script: A pre-production tool used to commit to paper all things seen or heard during the execution of the visual story.

sequence: A progressive series of scenes that relate to each other based on their common arc propelling content.

shape: A two-dimensional construct such as a square, triangle, or rectangle; like a line it has virtually no depth, only length and width.

shot: What the audience sees from the time the camera turns on until it reaches the next edit; a singular point of view.

shot list: A pre-production tool used to break down a storyboard into not just a series of actions, but a clear list of discreet pieces of footage as well.

showing versus telling: It is better to show than tell.

sidekick: A character who exists to give voice to the protagonist's deeper and sometimes more difficult feelings.

sincerity: A moment in the story where the audience truly believes that the character to whom it has been introduced chose a specific set of actions or exhibited a particular set of skills.

space: Refers to the imaginary three dimensions represented on a two-dimensional screen; it is the stage on which the action takes place on screen.

spatial relationships: Refers to the object's location in reference to another object or the camera.

staging: The arranging of three-dimensional forms to create an effective two-dimensional composition; in other words, the presentation of any element in such a way that the element is utterly clear.

stakes: The things that the characters stand to lose if they fail to attain their goals.

status quo: The normal state of people and locations before the change enters the story and forces action.

story: A fictional narrative whose goal is to clearly communicate ideas and feelings in an emotionally compelling manner. A story has a beginning, middle, and end (acts), and it follows the journey of a focal character as he encounters obstacles. His struggle with the obstacles results in a profound and external change in the character, obstacles, or both.

story arc: The process of a character facing his challenges and changing the world in order to overcome obstacles.

story beat: A singular moment in the story, usually taking the form of an action or reaction.

storyboard: A series of images that depict each significant action in a story.

straight-on: A shot in which the camera is level with the object it is shooting.

subjective camera: What the visual storyteller chooses to show and not show alters the meaning of the events onscreen.

supporting character: A character who exists to facilitate the hero's (main character's) journey or goal.

suspension of disbelief: The audience's willingness to pretend the lie it is presented with is true for the purpose of experiencing the story.

talent: A special, often creative or artistic aptitude, synonymous with ability.

tangible: Visible in reality and on screen.

tension: The emotion experienced by the audience while anticipating conflict.

through line: The series of obstacles (plot) that confront the empathic character and force him (and therefore the audience) to experience emotion, change, or both.

time: The fourth dimension.

time-based media: Media that must be viewed over time at the rate presented to the audience by the visual storyteller.

transition: A jump in continuity that moves the audience's perspective to the next action, which will reveal new meaning about the character or story.

universals: Feeling and experiences broad enough for nearly everyone in the audience to relate.

up-angle: When the camera is below the level of the subject and tilted up toward the object it is shooting.

visual storytelling: Both the art and the craft of sharing compelling characters and stories with an audience, in a visual medium.

world-building: Is the process of creating a consistent set of rules which serve as the reality in the world created by the visual storyteller.

index